Bake It Up!

Bake It Up! Desserts, Breads, Entire Meals & More

Rose Dunnington

LARK BOOKS
A Division of Sterling Publishing Co., Inc.
New York

Editor: Veronika Alice Gunter

Art Director: Robin Gregory

Cover Designer: Celia Naranjo

Stylist: Skip Wade

Photographer: Steven Mann

Design/Art Production: Thom Gaines

Art Production Assistant:

Bradley Norris

Editorial Assistance:

Delores Gosnell, Rose McLarney

Library of Congress Cataloging-in-Publication Data

Dunnington, Rose.
Bake it up! : desserts, breads, entire meals & more / by Rose Dunnington.
1st ed.
p. cm.
Includes index.
ISBN 1-57990-778-4 (hardcover)
1. Baking. 2. Desserts. 3. Bread. I. Title.
TX765.D86 2006
641.8'15—dc22

2006015072

10 9 8 7 6 5 4 3 2

Published by Lark Books, A Division of
Sterling Publishing Co., Inc.
387 Park Avenue South, New York, N.Y. 10016

Text © 2006, Rose Dunnington
Photography © 2006, Lark Books

Distributed in Canada by Sterling Publishing,
c/o Canadian Manda Group, 165 Dufferin Street
Ontario, Canada M6K 3H6

Distributed in the United Kingdom by GMC Distribution Services,
Castle Place, 166 High Street, Lewes, East Sussex, England BN7 1XU

Distributed in Australia by Capricorn Link (Australia) Pty Ltd.,
P.O. Box 704, Windsor, NSW 2756 Australia

If you have questions or comments about this book, please contact:
Lark Books
67 Broadway
Asheville, NC 28801
(828) 253-0467

Manufactured in China

ISBN 13: 978-1-57990-778-5
ISBN 10: 1-57990-778-4

For information about custom editions, special sales, premium and corporate purchases, please contact Sterling Special Sales Department at 800-805-5489 or specialsales@sterlingpub.com.

For Nadine Perry, my first and
best teacher. I love you, Mama!

Breakfast Fixins

Lunches, Dinners & More

Delicious Desserts

Breads You'll Love

You Know Why You Should Be Baking, Right?

Pop anything edible into the oven, and within minutes everyone within smelling distance is pulled to the source. It doesn't matter what's baking— bread, a pie, biscuits, a meal. A delicious smell fills the air and suddenly pets, brothers and sisters, parents, and long-lost friends show up. It's almost a party, and you're definitely the star.

Yes, baking is power. And I'm going to teach you how to master it—and make dozens of recipes for breakfasts, lunches, dinners, desserts, and more. You decide if you'll use your power for good, for yourself, for friends, for family, . . . whatever!

There are a few baking and cooking terms and techniques you'll need to know. You'll find them explained and demonstrated in the **Baking Basics** chapter. I'll show you just how easy it is to transform simple ingredients into fluffy muffins, flaky pie crust, and hearty meals.

I'll also share some tricks I learned in **culinary** school, and safety tips that are useful to beginners, accomplished cooks, and everyone in between.

To see photos of equipment you'll use, turn to the **Equipment Glossary** on page 106. I put cooking terms in bold (like **this**) throughout the book. You can look those words up in the glossary on page 108 if you need to.

So how about those recipes, anyway? I've divided them into four chapters, so you can find the perfect recipe for any occasion.

Start the day off deliciously with a selection from **Breakfast Fixins**. Since it may be difficult to choose which of my biscuit or muffin recipes to try first, maybe you should start

with a spicy sausage Strata Casserole or creamy dish of True Grits.

Make a meal from the **Lunches, Dinners & More** chapter, where you'll find Greek, Italian, Mexican, and American dishes, from Spanakofootballs and Holy Moly Stomboli to Hot Tamale Pie and Make It Your Way Pocket Pies.

Satisfy your sweet tooth with one of the mouthwatering goodies in the **Delicious Desserts** section. Want cheesecake? Ice-cream pie? Cookies? You've got more than a dozen options that will increase your personal fan club.

Or turn straight to the **Breads You'll Love** chapter and wow your friends and family with a homemade loaf of chewy, chunky Confetti Bread or a fruity, sweet batch of Stollen Goods, or whichever recipe suits your fancy.

You'll find how-to photos, stories about the recipes, ideas for experimenting, and helpful tips throughout the book. Here's the first tip: put on music before you get started so you won't get floury fingerprints on the buttons later. The second: Make enough to share, or put locks on the kitchen door, because once you start baking you'll be everyone's favorite person. Ready? **Bake it up!**

Baking Basics

First things first: wash your hands, tie back your hair if it's long, and put on an apron, if you want to. (I almost never wear an apron, but I don't mind floury handprints on my jeans.) If you're going to use your hands to mix or shape food, remove rings, bracelets, and watches.

Getting Started

After you choose what to make, read the recipe all the way through. The **yield** will tell you how much food it makes, such as "1 large pizza (6 to 8 slices)." The ingredients, equipment list, and instructions tell you what you use and what to do. Make sure you have everything you need and enough time to finish. Then stake out your territory. Arrange all of your equipment and ingredients on a countertop so you won't have to interrupt your work to find something. I like to put my ingredients all together on the left side of my work space. Once I've used an ingredient, I move the box or bag to the right so that I don't get confused and risk leaving an item out or adding it twice.

Ingredient Preparation

Some of the ingredients need to be prepped (prepared) before they are mixed with the other ingredients. Prepping ranges from taking butter out of the fridge and letting it warm to room temperature to washing, peeling, and slicing apples. Do the prep work first.

If liquid ingredients need to be heated, do it in the microwave or on the stovetop—whichever you do in your family. You can **soften** butter in the microwave, too, but make sure you do it on low power and check its progress every five seconds. (Often, the center of a stick of butter will melt before the outside is soft. Cut the butter into chunks to avoid this.) If the recipe calls for room temperature eggs, warm them by putting them in a bowl of hot water for five minutes. If ingredients should be cold, stick them in the freezer while you collect your equipment.

Wash and dry all **produce** in a **colander** before you use it. Plain water usually does the trick, but you can use a tiny drop of dish soap if you make sure to rinse well. **Peel** thin-skinned fruits and veggies with a **vegetable peeler**. Always peel away from your body.

Using Knives

Some of the prep work requires a knife and **cutting board**. Use a **chef's knife** or **paring knife** for produce, depending on the size of the food to be cut. Use a **serrated knife** for cutting bread. A **table knife** is perfect for cutting soft ingredients, such as butter.

Believe it or not, sharp knives are safer than dull ones. That's because you have to push harder with a dull knife, and the harder you push, the more chance there is for an accident. Wash a knife as soon as you're finished using it. NEVER put a knife in a sink full of soapy water—it might cut the next person (maybe you!) who reaches into the sink. Plus, banging against the sink can damage the knife.

To cut, make a claw out of the hand that you don't write with, tucking the thumb behind the fingertips. Your hand should look kind of like the letter "e" in sign language. Use that claw to hold down the food you're chopping. The thumb can guide the food forward, as long as it stays behind the fingers.

Never raise the **blade** (the cutting edge) of the knife higher than the knuckles of your guiding hand. Take your time and pay attention. If someone starts talking to you while you're using a knife, put it down while you have your conversation.

Slicing just takes one cut per piece of food. The thickness of a slice can vary according to the recipe and type of food. Try to make all the slices the same thickness. To slice bread, use a sawing motion and don't push too hard.

Dicing makes cubes with all six sides about the same size, so the finished recipe looks good and each bite has the same mix of flavors. What size? It depends on the recipe. When I say "dice," I mean

pieces of about ¾ inch on each side. "Small dice" just means cut them smaller. To dice, first slice the food to the correct thickness. Turn the slices and cut them into sticks. Turn again and cut the sticks into cubes.

To **mince** garlic or herbs into tiny, tiny pieces, put the food in a low pile on a big cutting board and use a long, sharp knife. Put your guiding hand on top of the knife, and chop, chop, chop.

Grate cheese, onions, and potatoes into small pieces with a **box grater**. Use a bigger hunk of food than you need for the recipe so your knuckles don't get too close to the sharp holes—your friends don't want to eat bloody foccacia! Push against the grater as you go down, but not when you go up. A little oil on the grater will keep cheese from sticking.

Measuring

When it comes to baking, you must measure carefully. Just use liquid measuring tools for liquids, and use solid measuring tools for solids.

Liquid measuring tools can be spoons or cups, and they usually have tons of lines and numbers, with cups, ml and oz beside the numbers. Put the cup on a stable surface and pour until you can see that the top of the liquid reaches the desired line.

Solid measuring tools can also be spoons and cups. Dip your scoop into the ingredient, then use the flat edge of a knife against the rim of the cup to push the extra off the top. If you use flour straight from the bag, stir it before you measure, to get the lumps out. Don't **pack** the ingredients unless the recipes calls for it. (Brown sugar for the cookie recipes is an ingredient I'll ask you

to pack when measuring.) It may seem as if the amounts of **baking soda** and **baking powder** are too tiny to do anything. Don't be fooled! These are the most powerful ingredients. Too much leaves a terrible taste in your food. Too little leaves food flat and dense.

Temperature is measured in degrees (abbreviated °). I use degrees Fahrenheit. It's important to **preheat** your oven so it will be at the correct temperature when you put your food in it.

Mixing

There are lots of different ways to mix ingredients. The most common one is stirring—making

circles in a bowl with a spoon. Here are some other mixing terms that I use:

Beat with an **electric mixer**, **whisk**, or fork. If you're using a whisk or fork, make small fast

circles with your wrist. Bring the utensil partially above the surface of the food so that air gets into the food.

Whipping is a faster and longer form of beating that makes it possible for ingredients to get super fluffy, such as for home-made whipped cream. I recommend using an electric beater or mixer for whipping, otherwise your arm will get really tired.

Cream softened butter and sugar by mixing with an electric mixer or fork. The mixture will get fluffy and lighter in color.

Fold ingredients into **batter** with a rubber spatula. Use a sideways stirring motion—think Ferris wheel. Scrape the batter from the bottom of the bowl and let it fall over the new ingredients.

Knead dough by pushing it with the heels of your hands onto a clean floured surface, such as a countertop, cutting board, or **pastry board**. Then fold the dough in half. Give the dough a quarter turn and knead it some more. Biscuits only need to be kneaded a few times, but you should knead bread a lot.

To **roll out** dough, such as pie crust, you'll need the dough, extra flour, a clean flat surface, and a

rolling pin. Sprinkle flour on the clean flat surface. Put the dough on the floured surface. Rub a little flour on the rolling pin, and starting in the middle of the dough and pushing out, begin rolling out the dough. Give the dough a quarter turn, and roll from the center again. Keep turning and rolling until the dough is the right thickness. If the dough gets sticky, add another sprinkle of flour.

Because bread making requires a few unique techniques, it gets its own how-to section on pages 84 to 89. (Followed by my **Breads You'll Love** recipes.)

Using an Oven

Make sure there's a rack in the middle of the oven before you pre-heat. And bake your marvelous creations as close to the center of the oven as you can for the most even cooking. (The muffin on the left was baked in the center, but the wonky one on the right was really close to the side.)

Set a **timer** for the shortest baking time indicated in the recipe.

Sticky Dough Tip

If the dough gets too sticky to work with, chill it. Cover the dough with plastic wrap, and refrigerate it, pastry board and all. After about 5 minutes of chilling, remove the dough from the fridge, uncover it, and roll it out some more.

When the timer goes off, look at your food through the oven door and compare how it looks to the recipe instructions. (Okay, this only works if you have a window in your oven. You may need to open the oven to check on the food.)

Baking Pans & Cookie Sheets

You can't just put Razzle Dazzle Pie or raw Chicken Fingers in the oven. They have to sit in or on something, right? Each recipe tells you what kind of equipment you'll need, including what to bake in.

You can make some variations. For instance, for the Faster, Sweeter, Breads on page 32, you can substitute muffin tins or mini-loaf pans for regular loaf pans. You'll need to adjust the cooking time, though. Smaller items cook faster than full-size loaves.

Greasing & Flouring

When a recipe calls for a **greased** pan, you need to apply some kind of butter, oil, or cooking spray to the pan before adding the food. The "grease" will make sure the food releases from the pan after baking. I like to grease a pan by rubbing it with a butter wrapper. If the recipe doesn't call for butter, I usually use unflavored cooking spray. Trust me. You don't want a "zesty Italian garlic" cake.

Flouring a pan is easy. After greasing it, sprinkle some flour in the pan. Then shake the pan side to side until the grease is coated.

Oven Mitts

Wear oven mitts when you take things out of the oven. Remember, the door and sides of the oven are hot too. Each recipe has an oven mitt on the page to remind you to protect yourself. Also, have a hot pad or trivet ready to put hot dishes on.

Cooling & Storage

Some baked goods need air to circulate around them as they cool, or they'll get soggy. Wear your oven mitts and flip cake, bread, or muffins out of their baking pans and onto a **wire cooling rack**. Use a metal spatula to move cookies, turnovers, or sandwich pockets onto a cooling rack.

Let your goodies cool completely before wrapping them for storage. Most baked goods should be stored at room temperature, but those with meat, cheese, or lots of eggs should be refrigerated. Of course, that's only in the unlikely event that you have leftovers!

Breakfast Fixins

For a delicious start to your school day or weekend, try a recipe from this chapter. If your time is limited, choose and make the recipe a day ahead so you can sleep in and eat on the go.

Tantalizing Turnovers

Why not try a fruit filled pastry for breakfast? This recipe uses two shortcuts from the freezer—puff pastry and frozen fruit.

makes 8 turnovers

ingredients

- 4 cups frozen peaches, blueberries, or raspberries
- 1/3 cup sugar
- 2 tablespoons cornstarch
- 1/2 teaspoon cinnamon (optional)
- 1 teaspoon vanilla extract
- dash of salt
- one 16-ounce package frozen puff pastry, thawed according to the directions on the box (Find this in your grocery's frozen foods section.)
- egg wash (See page 87.)

EQUIPMENT

- cutting board • mixing bowl
- wooden spoon • pastry brush or clean fingers • greased baking sheet

1. Preheat the oven to 400°F. Stir the fruit, sugar, cornstarch, cinnamon, vanilla, and salt together in the mixing bowl until well combined.

2. Cut both sheets of puff pastry into quarters, so you have eight equal squares. Brush egg wash along two connecting sides of each square.

3. Divide the fruit mixture among the squares. Fold each square of dough in half, forming a triangle, and pinch the edges closed. (It's okay to stretch the dough to make it fit over the filling.)

4. Put the turnovers on a greased baking sheet, at least 1/2 inch apart, and bake 15 to 20 minutes, or until golden brown.

Muffin Madness

What's your favorite kind of muffin? Use my simple blueberry muffin recipe below as a starter. If you want something unique, mix and match ingredients from the Goodie Bag on this page.

EQUIPMENT

- measuring cups and spoons
- 2 mixing bowls • fork • spoon
- greased or papered muffin tins

makes 12 to 16 muffins

ingredients

- 2 cups all-purpose flour, **sifted**
- ½ cup sugar
- 2 teaspoons baking powder
- ½ teaspoon salt
- 2 eggs
- ⅔ cup milk
- ¼ cup cooking oil
- 1 cup blueberries, rinsed and **picked**

1. Preheat the oven to 400°F. Combine the sifted flour, sugar, baking powder, and salt in one of the mixing bowls. If you're using a powdered spice, add it to the flour mixture. Stir until well blended.

2. Beat the eggs, milk, and oil together with a fork. If you're using an extract for flavoring, beat that in as well.

3. Dump the wet ingredients into the dry ingredients. Stir five times. Add the berries and stir until just combined. The batter should be clumpy and lumpy. For real. If it's smooth, your finished muffins will be dense. (Yuck.)

4. Fill the cups of the muffin tin two thirds of the way full, and bake 20 to 25 minutes. The baked muffins will come out of the pan more easily if you let them cool for a few minutes first.

Goodie Bag

- Add Spice: Choose 1 or 2 of these flavorings to include: ½ teaspoon of any kind of baking **extract**; ½ teaspoon ground cinnamon; ¼ teaspoon ground ginger, nutmeg, or allspice; ⅛ teaspoon ground cloves; 1 tablespoon finely ground lemon, lime, or orange **zest**; 2 tablespoons poppy seeds.
- Try a whole new flavor: Mix and match for a total of 1 cup, and let these items replace the blueberries in the recipe above: strawberries, rinsed, picked, and diced; apple, diced; shredded coconut; any kind of dried fruit, diced if necessary; any kind of nut (pecans, peanuts, etc.) in pieces; chocolate chips.

Strata Casserole

I combined recipes for an Italian dish called strata and my friend Julie's egg casserole and came up with this filling make-ahead breakfast. When you have a sleepover, get your friends to help you assemble the recipe at night so you all have something to look forward to in the morning.

EQUIPMENT

- toaster • table knife • measuring cups and spoons • greased baking dish, 9 x 9 or 8 x 9 inches • mixing bowl • whisk • plastic wrap
- weights, such as bags of flour, boxes of sugar, or dishes

makes 6 to 8 servings

ingredients

- 6 to 10 slices of sandwich bread, cut in half
- 2½ tablespoons butter, softened to room temperature
- 1 cup diced Polish sausage (sometimes called kielbasa)
- 2 cups packed fresh spinach leaves
- 2 cups grated Muenster cheese, divided in half
- 8 eggs
- 1 cup milk
- 1 to 2 teaspoons hot sauce, depending on your taste
- ½ teaspoon salt
- ¼ teaspoon ground pepper

1. Figure out how much bread you need by arranging half-pieces in the empty baking dish. You will need enough for two full layers. Toast the bread and butter both sides. (It's okay to be skimpy with the butter.)

2. Arrange one layer of buttered toast on the bottom of the greased baking dish. Sprinkle the sausage over it in an even layer. Now do a layer with the spinach. Top that with half of the cheese, saving the other half for the top. Finally, arrange the second layer of toast on top.

3. Whisk the eggs, milk, hot sauce, salt, and pepper together until well combined. Slowly pour this mixture over the stuff in the baking dish, letting it soak in as you pour. Sprinkle the remaining cheese on top.

4. Cover the dish loosely with plastic wrap. (Don't be skimpy with the wrap.) Weigh the top down so that the egg mixture will soak into the bread evenly. Use whatever you find that works, but don't use books because there's a slight chance that the egg will leak out. Put the whole shebang into the fridge overnight and go about your business. (Unfortunately, you can't indulge in my favorite sleepover pastime, making prank phone calls, because of caller ID. I hope the internet makes up for the loss.)

5. The next morning, preheat the oven to 350°F. Remove the weights and plastic wrap and bake the casserole for 55 to 60 minutes, or until it's golden brown and puffy.

Biscuit Bliss

The key to making outstanding biscuits is to use cold butter and handle the dough gently. Nudge the dough, don't force it. Sounds kinda Zen, right? Well, these biscuits do taste out-of-this-world good...

makes 15 little biscuits, 10 medium-sized ones, or 5 giants

ingredients

- 2 cups all-purpose flour
- 1 tablespoon baking powder
- 1 teaspoon salt
- ½ stick (¼ cup) cold butter, cut into chunks
- ½ to ¾ cup milk

1. Preheat the oven to 500°F. Stir the flour, baking powder, and salt together in the mixing bowl. Work the butter into the flour with your clean hands. This is done by rubbing your thumb against your fingertips, like you're making the gesture that means "money." (See photo A.) The final texture should be crumbly, sort of like uncooked instant oatmeal, with no obvious chunks of butter.

A

2. It's time to add the milk, but why didn't I give you an exact measurement? Well, the amount depends on how thoroughly the butter is blended with the flour. (The more they're blended, the less liquid is required to make dough.) It's a

continued on page 24 ····▶

B

little bit different every time. Start by adding ½ cup of milk to the butter/flour mixture, and stir with a wooden spoon. The goal is to make shaggy dough that pulls away from the sides of the bowl. (See photo B.) Add more milk a tiny bit at a time until you don't see any powdery flour but not so much that the dough gets really sticky. I usually end up using about ⅔ cup of milk.

C

3. Dump the dough out onto your lightly floured work surface. **Knead** the dough two to four times by gently pressing it with the heel of your hand (see photo C), then fold the dough in half. (See photo D.) Don't knead too much—just enough for the dough to change from shaggy to smooth. A little lumpiness is fine.

D

4. Gently pat the dough into a **round** about ½ inch thick. I often make the mistake of making the dough round thicker in the middle than at the edges, but that just makes for delicious biscuits that are a little bit lopsided. No biggie!

5. Cut out the biscuits by pressing the cutter straight down through the dough—don't twist as you cut. (See Biscuit Science on the next page to find out why.) Make your cuts as close together as you can. (See photo E.) Place the raw biscuits on the baking sheet, 1 inch apart if you like crispy sides as I do, or closer together if you like soft sides.

E

6. Repeat steps 4 and 5 with the scraps. Keep making biscuits until you've used all of your dough. After the biscuits bake, you'll notice that the ones made from scraps aren't quite as fluffy and tender as the ones you made first, but they're still yummy.

7. Bake the biscuits for 8 to 12 minutes. Small biscuits cook faster than large ones, so check on them sooner.

Biscuit Science

Why don't you twist the biscuit cutter? Strands of gluten join when they rub together. If you twist as you cut out the biscuits, the gluten on the sides of the biscuit makes a solid wall that holds the biscuit down instead of letting it rise in all of its fluffy glory.

So what's this gluten stuff, anyway? Gluten is a long protein made of two wheat proteins plus water. The more you mix and knead the dough, the longer the gluten strands get, forming a strong structure. Want to read more about the science of baking? Turn to Baking Science on page 88.

Turn the page for more biscuit recipes using the techniques you just read about.

TCB

These tomato cheese biscuits are almost too good. I mean, who could have imagined that anything could taste better than a regular hot buttered biscuit?

makes a dozen biscuits

ingredients

- 2 cups all-purpose flour
- 1 tablespoon baking powder
- 1 teaspoon salt
- $\frac{1}{2}$ teaspoon pepper
- $\frac{1}{2}$ stick ($\frac{1}{4}$ cup) butter, cut into chunks
- 1 cup grated sharp cheddar cheese
- $\frac{1}{2}$ to $\frac{3}{4}$ cup milk
- butter (optional)
- about 12 biscuit-size slices of tomato

1. Preheat the oven to 500°F. Stir the flour, baking powder, salt, and pepper together in the mixing bowl. Work the butter into the flour mixture with your fingers until the texture resembles uncooked instant oatmeal. (See step 1 and photo A on page 22 for detailed instructions.) Stir in the cheese. Add the milk to make shaggy dough that pulls away from the sides of the bowl. (See step 2 and photo B on page 24 for detailed instruction.)

2. Dump the dough out onto your lightly floured work surface and knead it two to four times. (See step 3 and photo C on page 24 for detailed instruction.) Gently pat the dough into a round about $\frac{1}{2}$ inch thick. Cut out the biscuits by pressing the cutter straight down through the dough. (See step 5 and photo E on page 24 for detailed instruction.) Place them on the baking sheet 1 inch apart. Use the dough scraps to make more. Bake for 8 to 12 minutes, or until golden brown.

3. As soon as they're cool enough to handle, split each biscuit in half, butter them if you want to, add a slice of tomato to each, and there you go—tomato cheese biscuit sandwiches. Eat 'em while they're hot.

Ask an Elvis Presley fan what TCB really stands for.

Layer Player

The exact same ingredients that make Biscuit Bliss on page 22 make these fancy biscuits that pull apart into layers of moist yummy goodness. So, what are you waiting for?

**makes 15 little biscuits,
10 medium-sized ones,
or 5 giants**

ingredients

- 2 cups all-purpose flour
- 1 tablespoon baking powder
- 1 teaspoon salt
- $1/2$ stick ($1/4$ cup) cold butter, cut into chunks
- $1/2$ to $3/4$ cup milk

1. Preheat the oven to 500°F. Stir the flour, baking powder, and salt together in the mixing bowl. Work HALF of the butter into the flour with your fingers until the mixture resembles uncooked instant oatmeal. (See step 1 and photo A on page 22 for detailed instruction.) Now work the other half of the butter in, but not all the way. You should still see lots of flat chunks of butter.

2. Add enough milk to make shaggy dough that pulls away from the sides of the bowl. I usually end up using about $2/3$ cup of milk. (See step 2 and photo B on page 24 for detailed instruction.)

3. Dump the dough out onto your lightly floured work surface. Pressing the heel of one hand into the dough, knead the dough one or two times, just enough to make it hold together.

4. Now the trick: roll the dough into a rectangle about $1/2$ inch thick. Fold the dough in thirds, as if you are folding a letter. (See photo.) Roll this smaller rectangle out until it's $1/2$ inch thick. Fold into thirds again, making these folds perpendicular to the first ones.) Do you see the layers developing? Roll and fold a total of four times, switching the direction of the folds each time. If the dough is hard to fold, let it rest a minute or two.

5. After the fourth fold, roll the dough to about 1 inch thick. Cut out the biscuits by pressing the cutter straight down through the dough—don't twist as you cut. (See photo E on page 24.) Place the raw biscuits onto the baking sheet, 1 inch apart if you like crispy sides, or closer together if you like soft sides.

6. Stack the dough scraps on top of each other, roll to 1 inch thick, and cut out more biscuits. Bake the biscuits for 8 to 12 minutes. Small biscuits cook faster than large ones, so check on them sooner.

True Grits

You might expect grits to have a sandy texture, because of their name. Actually, grits are creamy. When you add cheese and garlic . . . mmmm. I'm starting to drool just thinking about it. Stephanie, my mother-in-law, makes this dish for holiday breakfasts.

makes 6 to 8 servings

ingredients

- 4 cups water
- ½ teaspoon salt
- 1 cup uncooked quick grits
- 1½ cups grated cheddar cheese
- 1 tablespoon minced garlic
- ½ cup milk
- 1 stick (½ cup) butter, cut into chunks
- 2 eggs, lightly beaten

1. Preheat the oven to 325°F. Bring the water and salt to a boil in the pot on high heat on the stove top. Whisk in the grits, turn the burner down to medium, and boil 5 to 7 minutes, stirring occasionally.

2. Take the pot off the burner and add the cheese, garlic, milk, and butter. Stir until the cheese and butter are melted. **Temper** the eggs by stirring or whisking a big glop of hot grits into them. (See photo.) Add the tempered eggs to the pot of grits and stir until well combined.

3. Pour the mixture into the greased baking dish, scraping the inside of the pot with a rubber spatula to get every last bit. I like to get a helper to hold the heavy pot while I scrape. Bake 55 to 60 minutes, or until golden brown and slightly puffy. When your True Grits are ready, let them cool a bit before you dig in.

If you like, make some toast and cut a grapefruit in half while the grits bake. Put all three together for a delicious, filling breakfast.

Faster, Sweeter, Better Breads

Why buy breakfast breads when you can make them faster, sweeter, and better tasting at home? Try them hot from the oven, room temperature, or toasted and buttered.

EQUIPMENT

- measuring cups and spoons
- two mixing bowls • whisk •
rubber spatula • greased loaf
pan, 8 to 9 inches long
- table knife

makes 1 loaf per recipe

Call it Bananas
ingredients

- 1¾ cups all-purpose flour
- ½ cup packed brown sugar
- 2 teaspoons baking powder
- ½ teaspoon baking soda
- ½ teaspoon salt
- ½ teaspoon cinnamon

- 3 super-ripe bananas, mashed (about 1¼ cup)
- 2 eggs
- ¼ cup cooking oil
- ⅓ cup sour cream
- 1 teaspoon vanilla extract

Gad Zukes
ingredients

- 1¾ cups all-purpose flour
- 1 cup sugar
- 2 teaspoons baking powder
- ½ teaspoon baking soda
- ½ teaspoon salt

- 1 large zucchini, grated
- 3 eggs
- ¼ cup cooking oil
- 1 tablespoon finely grated orange zest

1. Preheat the oven to 350°F. Choose a recipe, and put all of its dry ingredients into one of the mixing bowls. (In these two recipes, the dry ingredients are on the left, and the wet ingredients are on the right.) Stir with a whisk until they are well combined and the flour isn't lumpy.

2. Put the wet ingredients in the other bowl and whisk until uniformly blended. Knock the whisk on the side of the bowl to shake off excess batter.

3. Dump the wet ingredients into the dry ingredients. Use a rubber spatula to combine them, making sure to incorporate the flour at the bottom of the bowl. Stop stirring when you no longer see any dry flour—a few lumps are fine, and over-mixing can make the bread tough.

4. Pour the batter into the greased loaf pan. Scrape the sides of the bowl with the rubber spatula to get every last bit. Bake 55 to 60 minutes until a wooden skewer poked in the middle comes out with a few moist crumbs but no sticky batter. Let the loaf cool for a few minutes. Run a table knife between the bread and the sides of the pan, and then flip the pan over (use oven mitts!) to release the loaf.

Cuppa Joe Cake

Coffee cake is deliciously sweet but not as rich as most cakes. That's how adults get away with eating it as an afternoon snack, with coffee to drink, of course. With a cuppa milk or juice, why not make this recipe as a breakfast treat for you?

EQUIPMENT

• measuring cups and spoons • two mixing bowls • whisk • rubber spatula • greased baking dish, 9 x 9 or 8 x 9 inches • table knife or wooden skewer

makes 9 delicious pieces

ingredients

Cake
- 1½ cups all-purpose flour
- ¾ cup sugar
- 1 teaspoon baking powder
- 1 teaspoon baking soda
- 1 cup sour cream
- 2 eggs
- 1 teaspoon vanilla extract

Cinnamon Swirl
- ½ cup packed brown sugar
- 1 tablespoon cinnamon

Streusel
- ⅓ cup sugar
- ½ stick butter, softened to room temperature
- ⅓ cup all purpose flour

1. Preheat the oven to 375°F. Put the dry ingredients (flour, sugar, baking powder, and baking soda) in one bowl and stir with a whisk to get the lumps out of the flour and combine the ingredients.

2. Put the wet ingredients (sour cream, eggs, and vanilla extract) in the other bowl and whisk until smooth. Dump the wet ingredients into the dry ingredients and stir with a rubber spatula until the flour is moistened, but the batter is still a bit lumpy. (Make sure you scrape the bottom of the bowl to incorporate all of the flour mixture.) Scrape the batter into the greased baking dish.

3. Combine the ingredients for Cinnamon Swirl. Sprinkle it on top of the cake, and use a table knife or wooden skewer to swirl it through the batter. (See photo.)

4. Mush the Streusel ingredients together with your fingers to make a paste. Drop raisin-sized pieces of streusel all over the top of the swirly batter.

5. Bake 30 to 35 minutes, or until the cake is golden brown and solid. Don't worry, Cuppa Joe Cake is delicious even if you underbake or overbake it a little bit.

Pecan Sticky Rolls

makes 6 to 8 sweet servings

ingredients

- 3 cups all-purpose flour
- ¼ cup sugar
- 1 packet (2¼ teaspoons) active dry yeast
- ½ teaspoon salt
- 2 eggs, lightly beaten
- ½ stick (1/4 cup) butter, melted
- ½ cup milk
- ½ stick (¼ cup) butter
- ¼ cup sugar
- 1 tablespoon ground cinnamon
- ½ cup packed brown sugar
- 2 tablespoons water
- 1 cup pecans

To increase your chance of being allowed to make these gooey, nutty treats as regular breakfast buns, share them with your parents.

1. Stir the flour, ¼ cup sugar, yeast, and salt together until thoroughly combined. Add the eggs, melted butter, and milk, and stir until all of the flour is evenly moistened. Dump the dough out on your pastry board. Knead the dough until it forms a somewhat smooth ball. This dough is really sticky and soft, but try not to use too much extra flour when you knead (use less than ¼ cup). Since you use all-purpose flour, this dough won't get smooth and satiny like bread dough. It will have small lumps. Rinse the mixing bowl with hot water. Put the dough in the bowl, cover it with a towel, and let **rise** in a warm place until **doubled** in size, about one hour.

2. Meanwhile, microwave the brown sugar, water, and remaining half stick of butter for 5 seconds, or until the butter is melted. Stir this concoction until smooth, and then pour it into the bottom of the baking dish. (Careful, it's hot.) Sprinkle the pecans in an even layer over the sauce. Preheat the oven to 350°F. Stir the cinnamon and remaining ¼ cup sugar together. **Punch** down the dough and transfer it to the pastry board. Roll out the dough into a rectangle about ¼ inch thick.

3. Sprinkle the cinnamon sugar on the dough. Starting at the long side, roll the dough into a log. Then pinch the dough together, making a seam. Use the thread to cut the log into 1-inch slices. (See photo.) Arrange the slices on top of the pecans in the baking dish. It's okay if they don't touch each other. Bake 20 to 25 minutes.  The tops of the spirals should be darker than raw dough, but still pretty pale.

4. The last step is tricky. Get an adult to help if you're at all uncomfortable doing this. As soon as the hot Pecan Sticky Rolls come out of the oven, put the serving plate upside down on top of the baking dish. Using oven mitts, flip the baking dish over so that the plate is on the bottom. Remove the baking dish and let the rolls cool for a few minutes before you gobble them up.

Lunches, Dinners & More

Count on the recipes in this chapter for filling, hearty foods that make great snacks and meals.

Hot Tamale Pie

Okay, so this isn't a pie. It's not tamales, either. Don't let that stop you, though, because it's still an incredibly delicious baked chicken and salsa concoction.

1. Preheat the oven to 375°F. Pull the skin off the chicken and discard the skin. Shred the chicken meat into small pieces with your fingers.

2. Stir the chicken and salsa together until well combined and transfer it to the baking dish. Sprinkle the cheese in an even layer over the chicken mixture.

3. Stir the cornmeal into 1 cup of the water. Heat the remaining 2½ cups of water with the salt on the stove top on high until it starts to bubble. Reduce the heat to medium and pour in the cornmeal mixture, whisking as you pour. The next 5 to 10 minutes of your life will be devoted to whisking. Whisk the mixture constantly as it cooks to avoid lumps or scorching. As soon as the mixture bubbles, turn the heat down to low. Continue cooking and whisking until the mush has thickened to the consistency of mashed potatoes.

4. Get your helper to tilt the pot over the baking dish while you use a rubber spatula to scrape the mush onto the casserole. It's really too difficult to do this yourself, because you can easily burn yourself on the pot or drop it, so do use a helper. Smooth the top of the mush, making sure to go all the way to the edges of the dish. Cover with foil and bake 30 minutes. Remove the foil and bake another 15 to 20 minutes, or until the top is slightly browned.

makes 8 to 10 servings

ingredients

- one cooked chicken, about 1½ pounds (24 ounces) (I buy a rotisserie chicken).
- 16-ounce jar salsa verde (also called green salsa or tomatillo salsa)
- 1½ cups grated Monterey Jack cheese
- 3½ cups water, divided
- ¾ teaspoon salt
- 1 cup cornmeal

Give Pizza a Chance

Pizza has it all—fun to make, fun to eat, and you can customize it with your favorite toppings. I made this one half pepperoni, half veggies. Which side would you choose?

EQUIPMENT

- measuring cups and spoons • 2 mixing bowls • wooden spoon • lightly floured pastry board • extra flour for kneading • clean kitchen towel • greased pizza pan • rubber spatula • pizza cutter or serrated knife

makes 1 large pizza (6 to 8 slices)

ingredients

- 3¼ cups bread flour
- 1 packet (2¼ teaspoons) active dry yeast
- ½ teaspoon salt
- 2 tablespoons olive oil
- 1⅓ cups water, the temperature of a warm bath
- another splash of olive oil, about 1 tablespoon
- 2 to 3 cups tomato sauce
- 3 to 4 cups grated mozzarella cheese
- your choice of toppings (meat toppings must be precooked)

1. Stir the flour, yeast, and salt together in the mixing bowl. Add the warm water and olive oil. Mix until you have shaggy dough. Dump the dough onto the pastry board and knead 4 to 5 minutes, until it is a smooth, springy ball.

2. Put a splash of olive oil in the second mixing bowl. Put the dough in the bowl, slop it around, flip it over, and slop it around some more, so the dough is lightly coated with olive oil. Cover the dough in the bowl with a kitchen towel, and let it **rise** until **doubled** in size, about one hour.

3. Preheat the oven to 425°F. **Punch** the dough down and shape it into a flat disc. Make two fists and put the dough on top of them. Move your fists in little up-and-down circles. The dough will slowly rotate over your fists and stretch out into a larger circle. (See photo.) It's easy, and it doesn't have to look perfect.

4. Place the dough in the pizza pan and use your fingers to push it all the way to the edges of the pan. Spread the tomato sauce on the pizza with the rubber spatula. Scatter your toppings on the sauce. Sprinkle cheese over the whole shebang. Bake 20 to 25 minutes, or until the cheese is melted and the crust is golden brown. Let the pizza cool off some before you slice and eat it—pizza burn on the roof of your mouth is horrible.

Chicken Fingers

Satisfy the munchies with this popular snack. Since these chicken fingers are baked, they're way healthier than the fast food kind. Don't worry! They still taste great!

EQUIPMENT

• colander • paper towels • greased baking sheet • 2 shallow dishes (I use pie plates.) • measuring cups and spoons • fork • tongs • serving plate

makes 3 to 5 servings

ingredients

- 1 pound chicken tenders (The package might call them "loins.")
- 1 cup flour
- 1 teaspoon salt
- ½ teaspoon pepper
- ¼ teaspoon baking powder
- 1 egg
- cooking spray
- Honey Baby Sauce (See recipe this page.)

Honey Baby Sauce

Combine ¼ cup honey with ¼ cup spicy brown mustard in a small bowl.

1. Preheat the oven to 375°F. Rinse the chicken under running water in the colander, and blot it dry with the paper towels. The drying part is important because the coating won't stick to wet chicken, so don't skip it.

2. Combine the dry ingredients in one of the shallow dishes. Use the fork to mix them together.

3. Use the fork to beat the egg lightly in the other shallow dish. Now the fun part: you **dredge** each piece of chicken first in the flour (shake off any extra), then in the egg, and then back in the flour. (See photo.) Finally, place the chicken on the baking sheet. Lightly spray the tops of the dredged chicken with oil.

4. Bake for 15 minutes. Then slide the baking sheet out of the oven, and flip the chicken pieces over with the tongs. Lightly spray them with oil, and bake another 5 to 10 minutes, or until golden brown.

5. Let the chicken fingers cool, and put them on a serving plate before you dip them in Honey Baby Sauce. Chow down.

Spanakofootballs

These savory treats are based on the Greek dish, spanakopita. I kept the first part of the name, which means "spinach," and dropped the "pita," which means "pie." Why "footballs"? Well, back in the old days before text messaging, we passed notes in class on actual paper. This triangular fold was known as the football.

EQUIPMENT

• measuring cups and spoons
• mixing bowl • rubber spatula or wooden spoon • large cutting board • pastry brush • paring knife or round pizza cutter • baking sheet

makes 10 fabulous footballs

ingredients

- 10-ounce package of frozen chopped spinach, thawed
- 4 ounces feta cheese, crumbled (about 1 cup)
- 1 cup ricotta cheese
- 1 egg
- 1 tablespoon minced garlic
- ½ teaspoon black pepper
- 8-ounce package frozen phyllo dough, thawed according to the directions on the box (Find this in your grocery's frozen foods section.)
- ¾ stick of butter (6 tablespoons), melted

1. Preheat the oven to 400°F. Squeeze the water out of the spinach and put it in the mixing bowl (the spinach, not the water). Add the feta, ricotta, egg, garlic, and pepper and stir until well combined.

2. Put one sheet of phyllo on the cutting board and brush it all over with melted butter, making sure that you don't skimp at the edges. (See photo.) Line up another sheet of phyllo on top of that and brush with butter. Don't worry about a few wrinkles or tears. Do a third layer the same way, phyllo and butter.

3. Cut the three layers of phyllo in half lengthwise. Spoon about ¼ cup of the spinach/cheese filling onto one end of each rectangular strip of phyllo. Starting at the end with the filling, fold the phyllo over the filling to make a triangle. (See photo.) Continue folding until you have a neat triangular football of yum. If there's a bit of extra phyllo hanging off the side, fold once more so that the extra is on the bottom. Do the same thing with the other strip and place the two footballs on a baking sheet ½ inch apart.

4. Repeat steps 2 and 3 until you've used all of your filling. Brush melted butter on top of your goodies. Bake them for 15 to 20 minutes, or until the corners are brown and crispy and the tops are golden. Don't flick these footballs—eat them!

Real Man's Quiche

In the 1980s quiche got the reputation of being fussy, prissy food. Maybe because its name is French and some people felt stupid because they didn't know how to pronounce it. (It's easy: keesh.) Luckily, that ridiculous attitude went out with cassette tapes.

EQUIPMENT

- measuring cups and spoons
- food processor • chilled mixing bowl • plastic wrap • pastry board
- rolling pin • greased pie plate
- kitchen shears or paring knife
- mixing bowl • spoon
- aluminum foil

makes 1 quiche (6 servings)

ingredients

- 1 Perfecto Pie Crust (See page 76.)
- 1½ to 2 cups veggies, chopped into bite-sized pieces (I use broccoli.)
- ½ to 1 cup cooked meat, chopped into bite-sized pieces (I use turkey bacon.)
- 1½ cups grated cheese (I use cheddar.)
- 1½ cups milk, heated until it steams but doesn't boil
- 3 eggs, lightly beaten
- ⅛ to ¼ teaspoon salt (use less with salty meats such as bacon or ham)
- ⅛ teaspoon ground nutmeg
- ⅛ teaspoon black pepper
- dash hot sauce (optional)

1. Preheat the oven to 375°F. Fill the unbaked pie crust with the veggies, meat, and cheese.

2. Combine the milk, eggs, salt, nutmeg, pepper, and hot sauce. Pour the mixture over the goodies in the pie crust.

3. Bake 35 minutes. Check to see if the edge of the crust is browned. If it is, loosely cover the quiche with foil so the crust doesn't burn. Bake another 10 to 15 minutes, or until the bottom crust is browned and the middle of the quiche barely jiggles when you shake it. (Of course you'll only be able to see if the bottom is browned if you use a glass pie plate.)

4. Remove the quiche from the oven. Let the quiche cool for at least 15 minutes before you cut it into servings.

Make It Your Way
Pocket Pies

Pocket pies combine the deliciousness of potpies with the ease of finger food. Best of all, you can fill them with your favorite combination of veggies, cheeses, and meats.

EQUIPMENT

• chef's knife • vegetable peeler • measuring cups and spoons • mixing bowl • wooden spoon • pastry board • rolling pin • salad plate or sauce pan lid about 6 inches in diameter (optional) • paring knife • pastry brush • fork • lightly greased baking sheet

makes 6 pocket pies

ingredients

- 2 cups diced diced deli meat of your choice (I used turkey.)
- 1 carrot, peeled and sliced into ¼-inch rounds (about ½ cup), (optional)
- 1 cup frozen peas (you could substitute corn, or try half of each)
- ¼ teaspoon black pepper
- one 10-ounce can condensed cream of potato soup, undiluted
- one recipe Perfecto Pie Crust (See page 76.)
- egg wash (See page 87.)
- 6 slices provolone cheese (or cheese of your choice)

1. Preheat the oven to 425°F. Stir the meat, vegetables, pepper, and soup together in the mixing bowl until well combined. Divide the pie crust into six equal parts.

2. **Roll out** each part separately until about ¼ inch thick. If you want a perfect circle, lightly place a salad plate or small sauce pan lid on top of the dough and trim around it with a paring knife.

3. Brush egg wash around the edge of a dough round. Place a slice of cheese onto the middle of the round and top it with ½ to ⅔ cup of the filling mixture. Fold the dough over the filling so you have a half circle. Press the sides closed with a fork. Move the pocket pie onto the baking sheet. Use the paring knife to cut a small **slash** in the top to allow steam to escape while it bakes.

4. Repeat steps 2 and 3 for the remaining dough and filling. Bake 35 to 40 minutes, or until golden brown. Remove the pocket pies from the oven and let them cool a bit before you take a bite or pack them to go. (The filling is incredibly hot when it first comes out of the oven, and the pockets will get soggy if you wrap them before they cool.)

These are easy to pack and taste great hot or cold. So why not save a few for tomorrow's lunch or after school snack?

Holy Moly Stromboli

The last time I made this recipe, I planned to give one whole stromboli to my friend Mike for his birthday. My husband got tears in his eyes when he learned that he wouldn't get to eat both strombolis. This recipe is that good.

EQUIPMENT

- measuring cups and spoons
- mixing bowl • wooden spoon
- lightly floured pastry board
- clean kitchen towel • rolling pin
- greased baking sheet • pastry brush • serrated knife

1. Stir the flour, yeast, and salt together in the mixing bowl. Add the warm water and olive oil. Mix until you have shaggy dough. Dump the dough onto the pastry board and knead 4 to 5 minutes until it is a smooth, springy ball.

2. Rinse and dry the mixing bowl. Put a splash of olive oil in it. Put the dough in the bowl, slop it around, flip it over, and slop it around some more so the dough is lightly coated with olive oil. Cover the dough in the bowl with a kitchen towel, and let it **rise** until **doubled** in size, about one hour.

3. Preheat the oven to 425°F. **Punch** down the dough and divide it in half. Working on the pastry board, **roll out** one part of the dough into a rectangle about 8 by 12 inches. If the dough keeps shrinking up instead of rolling out, let it rest a couple minutes and try again.

4. Layer half of the cheese, meats, and peppers in a line down the middle of the dough rectangle. Fold the sides and ends of the dough over the fillings, making a rectangular package. Pinch the edges together to seal the package. Put the stromboli on the baking sheet with the seam side down. Brush the top with egg wash. Make slashes with the serrated knife to allow steam to escape while it bakes.

5. Repeat steps 3 and 4 with the remaining dough and fillings. Bake 20 to 25 minutes, or until golden brown. Serve slices of stromboli with the warm marinara sauce. (The sauce is for dipping.) Remember to share—I don't want anyone else crying over this recipe!

makes 2 strombolis of 2 to 4 servings each

ingredients

- 3¼ cups bread flour plus extra for kneading
- 1 packet (2¼ teaspoons active dry yeast
- ½ teaspoon salt
- 2 tablespoons olive oil
- 1⅓ cups water, the temperature of a warm bath
- another splash of olive oil, about 1 tablespoon
- 8 ounces mozzarella cheese, sliced
- 8 ounces sliced salami
- 8 ounces sliced smoked ham
- 10-ounce jar roasted red peppers, drained (optional)
- egg wash (See page 87.)
- about 2 cups marinara sauce, warmed

Tater Torte

It's awesome to have cake for dinner. This is kind of a fake-out though — it tastes like twice-baked potatoes and is more nutritious than cake.

EQUIPMENT

• vegetable peeler • chef's knife
• large pot • fork • colander • measuring cups and spoons • potato masher • rubber spatula
• 9-inch springform cake pan, greased (Make sure the latch is in the closed position.)
• wooden skewer • table knife

1. Put the potatoes and garlic in the pot with enough water to cover them by at least 2 inches, but leave at least 3 inches of empty space at the top to avoid boiling-over disasters. Bring the water to a boil on high, then reduce the heat to medium and boil 15 to 20 minutes, or until the potatoes are soft enough to easily stab with a fork.

2. Preheat the oven to 350°F. Drain the potatoes and garlic in the colander in the sink and return them to the empty pot. (Get an adult to do this if the pot's too heavy or you're feeling lazy.) Add the butter, sour cream, milk, salt, pepper, and horseradish. Mash until smooth. **Temper** the eggs by stirring some of the hot mashed potatoes into them, then add the egg mixture to the potatoes and stir until well combined.

3. Put the bread crumbs into the greased springform pan and tilt it until the bottom and sides are coated. Dump out the extra bread crumbs and save them for the top.

4. Slop half of the potato mixture into the pan and spread it into an even layer with the rubber spatula. Make a cheddar "frosting" layer (see photo). Then add the rest of the potato mixture, again smoothing the top with the rubber spatula. Sprinkle the remaining bread crumbs on top. Bake 55 to 60 minutes, or until a wooden skewer poked in the middle comes out clean.

5. Let the Tater Torte rest 10 minutes. Then run a knife between the torte and the sides of the pan. Release the latch on the side of the pan slowly, watching for cracks. If you see any cracks, use the knife to unstick the cake from the pan at that spot. Gently wiggle the pan away, up, and off of the cake.

6. Decorate your fabulous creation with any of the optional toppings. I made mine look like a birthday cake 'cuz I'm cheesy like that.

makes 8 to 12 servings

ingredients

- 2½ pounds Russet potatoes, peeled and cut into 2-inch chunks
- 2 cloves garlic, peeled
- 2 tablespoons butter
- ½ cup sour cream
- ½ cup milk
- 1½ teaspoon salt
- 1 teaspoon ground pepper
- 2 tablespoons prepared horseradish
- 5 eggs, lightly beaten
- ⅓ cup bread crumbs
- 1 cup grated cheddar cheese
- optional toppings: sour cream, chives, crumbled bacon, grated cheddar

Lilly's Creamed Corn Cornbread

My sister Lilly contributed this yummy recipe to a cookbook her second grade class created. Most parents probably didn't let their kids use an iron skillet, but if you can, your cornbread will have a perfect crust.

makes 6 to 8 servings

ingredients

- 3 eggs, lightly beaten
- 1½ cup cornmeal
- 14-ounce can of creamed corn
- 1½ cups sour cream
- ½ cup cooking oil plus 2 tablespoons for cooking in the pan
- ¾ teaspoon salt
- 1 tablespoon baking powder

1. Put the skillet in the oven and preheat to 350°F. (Preheating the iron skillet is the secret to getting a perfectly browned, crunchy crust. Cast iron skillets are really heavy. You might want to get an adult to deal with the hot pan, even though you're not in second grade.) If you are using a baking pan, just preheat the oven and go to step 2.

2. Stir all of the ingredients together (reserving the extra oil for the skillet) in the mixing bowl until well combined. Choose a place to set the hot skillet, because you are about to take it out of the oven.

3. Wearing the oven mitts, take the hot skillet out of the oven and set it down. Add the 2 tablespoons of oil to the skillet. Pour the batter into the skillet, then place the skillet back in the oven. Bake 40 to 45 minutes or until the top is a crunchy yellowish brown. Remove the skillet from the oven, and put an oven mitt over the handle so no one touches it. It will stay hot for a long time. Cut the cornbread into wedges to serve.

Tex-Mex Variation

Looking for spice? Transform this recipe into a Tex-Mex Cornbread. When you get to step 2, just add 1 mild banana pepper, diced small (remove the seeds); 1 jalapeño pepper, minced (include the seeds if you want extra heat); and 1 cup grated cheddar cheese. Wash your hands right after you handle hot peppers, and don't touch your eyes or face.

Delicious Desserts

Look no further for easy recipes to make scrumptious brownies, cookies, cakes, pies, cobblers, and more. This desserts chapter has it all.

Spectacular Strawberry Shortcake (Sx3) is sooo yummy— and not really that short. Especially when you pile on the homemade whipped cream.

1. Preheat the oven to 500°F. Stir the flour, ¼ cup of sugar, baking powder, and salt together in the mixing bowl. Use your clean fingers or a spoon to work the butter into the flour mixture until the texture resembles uncooked instant oatmeal. (See page 22 for detailed instructions on making dough.) Add the milk and stir briefly to make shaggy dough that pulls away from the sides of the bowl.

(See page 22 for detailed instructions on making dough.)

EQUIPMENT

- measuring cups and spoons
- 2 mixing bowls • wooden spoon
- lightly floured pastry board
- large biscuit or cookie cutter
- baking sheet • chef's knife
- serving spoon

2. Dump the dough out onto your lightly floured work surface and **knead** it two to four times. Gently pat the dough into a **round** about ½ inch thick. Cut out the shortcakes by pressing the cutter straight down through the dough. Place the shortcakes on the baking sheet 1 inch apart. Use the dough scraps to make more. Bake for 10 to 12 minutes.

3. While the shortcakes are baking, taste a strawberry slice. How much of the 1 to 2 tablespoons of sugar do your berries need? Mix that amount with the berries in the bowl.

4. Take the baked shortcakes out of the oven. For each serving, cut a shortcake in half horizontally. Spoon strawberries over the bottom half, followed by a dollop of whipped cream. Top it with the top of the shortcake, and garnish with more strawberries and whipped cream.

Once you master this recipe, try using raspberries, sliced peaches, or kiwi instead of strawberries. Tastes deliciously different, right?

makes 5 to 6 shortcakes

ingredients

- 2 cups all-purpose flour
- ¼ cup sugar
- 1 tablespoon baking powder
- ½ teaspoon salt
- ½ stick of butter (¼ cup), sliced about ¼ inch thick
- ½ to ¾ cup milk
- 2 pints fresh strawberries, washed, hulled, and sliced about ¼ inch thick
- 1 to 2 tablespoons sugar
- 1 batch of whipped cream (See step 2 on page 74.)

Cobbler Gobbler

My favorite cobbler fruit combo is peaches and blueberries, but you can make it with whatever fruit you want. Um, maybe not grapefruit.

makes 6 servings

ingredients

- 4 to 6 peaches, peeled and sliced
- 1 pint blueberries, washed and picked over
- 1 cup sugar
- 3 tablespoons cornstarch
- pinch of salt
- 1 teaspoon vanilla extract
- 2 cups all-purpose flour
- 1/4 cup sugar
- 1 tablespoon baking powder
- 1/2 teaspoon salt
- 1/4 cup candied ginger, minced (optional)
- 1/2 stick butter (1/4 cup), cut into 1/4-inch slices
- 3/4 to 1 cup milk

1. Preheat the oven to 400°F.
Combine the peaches, blueberries,
1 cup of sugar, cornstarch, pinch of salt,
and vanilla extract. Stir until all of the cornstarch dissolves.
Dump the fruit mixture into the baking dish.

2. Stir the flour, 1/4 cup sugar, baking powder, salt, and candied ginger together. Work the butter into the flour with your fingers until the texture is crumbly. Then add enough milk to make shaggy, sticky dough. (This dough should be slightly goopier than normal biscuit dough. If you need detailed instructions, turn to page 22.)

3. Use a spoon to drop the dough on top of the fruit in the baking dish. (See photo.) Cobbler got its name because it looks like lumpy, bumpy cobblestone streets, so don't smooth it out. Bake 35 to 40 minutes, or until the top is golden brown and the juices are bubbling around the

edges. Then remove your cobbler from the oven and let the food cool a bit. I like to serve fresh cobbler with ice cream.

Ultimate Brownies

These brownies are fudgy, moist, and loaded with rich chocolate flavor. Make them from the basic recipe or try one of the scrumptious variations. You won't be disappointed.

makes 15 squares of deliciousness

ingredients
- 1 stick (1/2 cup) butter
- 4 squares (4 ounces) unsweetened baking chocolate
- 2 tablespoons cocoa powder
- 3 eggs
- 1 cup sugar
- 1 cup packed brown sugar
- 1/4 teaspoon salt
- 1 teaspoon vanilla extract
- 1 cup all-purpose flour, **sifted**

1. Preheat the oven to 350°F. Put the butter, unsweetened chocolate, and cocoa powder in the microwave-safe bowl and microwave on high about 2 minutes until the butter is melted. Whisk this until the chocolate has melted and the mixture is smooth. Let it cool. (Don't have a microwave? Heat the ingredients in a small pan over low heat, stirring with whisk until melted and smooth.)

2. Whisk the eggs, sugar, brown sugar, salt, and vanilla in the mixing bowl until well combined and somewhat fluffy. Whisk in the cooled chocolate mixture (use a rubber spatula to get every last bit) until mostly combined—you should still see streaks of colors.

3. Fold the sifted flour into the batter with the rubber spatula until well combined. Pour the batter into the greased baking dish. Use the rubber spatula to scrape down the bowl and smooth the top of the batter. Bake 35 to 40 minutes.

4. Let the brownies cool before you cut them into squares or they'll be really crumbly. Yeah, right! I can never wait that long.

Looking for variety?

- Make your brownies Nutty by adding a cup of chopped pecans when you fold in the flour.
- For a taste that's Cheesecake-y, combine one 8-ounce package of softened cream cheese, 1 egg, and 1/4 cup sugar. Dollop spoonfuls of this mixture on the brownie batter in the baking dish. Use a rubber spatula to swirl it in.

I  Gingerbread

Do you like soft, spicy, sweet gingerbread? Then you'll LOVE this cake. I can't take all the credit: it's my friend Lynn's luscious lemon glaze that makes this dessert irresistible.

EQUIPMENT

- measuring cups and spoons
- 2 mixing bowls • electric mixer • fork
- rubber spatula • lightly greased 9 by 13-inch baking dish, or a Bundt pan • wooden skewer

makes 1 outstanding cake (about 12 slices)

ingredients
- 1 stick (½ cup) butter, softened to room temperature
- ½ cup sugar
- 1 egg
- 2½ cups all-purpose flour
- 1½ teaspoons baking soda
- ½ teaspoon salt
- 1 to 2 teaspoons ground ginger
- ½ to 1 teaspoon ground cinnamon
- ¼ to ½ teaspoon ground nutmeg
- 1 cup dark molasses
- 1 cup hot water
- 1 cup powdered sugar
- juice of 1 lemon

1. Preheat the oven to 350°F. Cream the butter and sugar with the electric mixer until evenly colored and fluffy. Add the egg and beat until even fluffier.

2. Combine the flour, baking soda, and spices in the other bowl. Stir them with a fork until well blended. Combine the molasses and water in a large measuring cup.

3. With the mixer on low, add about a third of the flour mixture to the creamed mixture. When that's all blended in, add half of the molasses mixture, and beat until well blended. Beating between additions, add half the remaining flour mixture, then the rest of the molasses mixture, then the rest of the flour mixture. Set the electric mixer aside and use the rubber spatula to scrape the sides and bottom of the bowl and make sure all of the ingredients are well blended. (Don't worry—it's supposed to bubble like that!) Scrape the batter into the baking dish or Bundt pan, and bake 55 to 60 minutes, or until a wooden skewer poked in the thickest part comes out with only a few crumbs stuck to it.

4. While the cake bakes, make the glaze. Combine the powdered sugar and lemon juice in a liquid measuring cup and beat with a fork until smooth. When the cake is done, remove it from the oven. If you baked your cake in a baking dish, just pour the glaze on top and cut servings straight from the dish. If you used a Bundt pan, let the cake rest for 5 minutes after you take it from the oven, then flip it onto a serving plate (use your oven mitts if the pan is still hot), remove the pan, and drizzle the glaze over it. Either way—yum-o!

For Goodness Cake!

Impress your friends with this fabulous chocolate cake. You don't have to tell them how easy it was to make.

makes 10 to 12 slices

ingredients

- 2⅔ cups cake flour, sifted (You can use 2½ cups all-purpose if you don't have cake flour.)
- 1½ cups sugar
- ¾ teaspoon salt
- 2¼ teaspoons baking powder
- 3 eggs, lightly beaten
- ¾ cup milk
- 2 teaspoons vanilla extract
- 1½ sticks (¾ cup) butter, cut into chunks and softened to room temperature
- 1 pint heavy cream
- ½ stick (¼ cup) butter
- 1½ cups semi-sweet mini-chocolate chips

EQUIPMENT

- measuring cups and spoons • 2 mixing bowls • electric mixer • rubber spatula
- 3 greased and floured round 9-inch cake pans • wooden skewer
- cooling rack • small saucepan
- whisk • icing spatula, rubber spatula, or table knife

1. Preheat the oven to 350°F. Stir the flour, sugar, salt, and baking powder together in the mixing bowl. Add the eggs, milk, and vanilla and beat on low until the dry ingredients are moistened. Turn the mixer up to medium-high (medium if it's a standing mixer) and beat for 1 minute. Continue beating as you add the chunks of butter one at a time. Beat an additional 1 to 2 minutes until the batter is light in color and fluffy.

2. Divide the batter among the three cake pans, using the rubber spatula to scrape every bit from the bowl. Smooth the cake batter with the rubber spatula. Bake 20 to 25 minutes until a wooden skewer poked in the middle of a cake comes out with only a few crumbs on it. Remove the pans from the oven. Let the cakes cool for 5 minutes, then flip them onto a cooling rack and remove the pans. Don't forget your oven mitts! Make sure your cake has cooled completely before you frost it.

continued on page 66 ····➤

3. Make the frosting while the cake is baking. Heat the cream and remaining 1/2 stick of butter in the sauce pot on medium, stirring occasionally with the whisk. Put the mini-chocolate chips in a mixing bowl. When the cream is steamy and the butter is mostly melted, pour it over the chocolate chips. Whisk this mixture until the chips are melted and the color is the same throughout—no speckles. Chill the chocolate mixture (called **ganache**) until it's as firm as sour cream.

4. When the ganache is cold, whip it with the electric mixer on high until lighter in color and very thick and fluffy. (It only works if the ganache is cold, so don't skip that step.)

5. Put the cake together: First stack the cake layers with frosting in between them. (See photo.) Next, cover the whole cake with a thin layer of frosting. (This is called the **crumb layer**.) Don't worry about how it looks at this point. Put the cake in the freezer for 5 minutes until the crumb  layer has hardened and trapped the crumbs. Now you can add the rest of that beautiful frosting. Experiment making swirls in the frosting with the spatula or table knife. Serve your masterpiece at room temperature, but store leftovers in the fridge. Leftovers …yeah, right!

Minicakes = Cupcakes

You can use my cake recipe to make cupcakes. Just line the cups of a muffin tin with paper cupcake liners, fill each two-thirds full of cake batter, and bake 15 to 20 minutes. Slap some frosting on top of the cooled cupcakes and you've got a party waiting to happen. Flip back a page to get started...

Say Cheesecake

Ignore the hype: cheesecakes are easy to make. The hard part is waiting for them to bake and cool. Here's my recipe for a traditional cream cheese cheesecake. It'll put a smile on your face.

EQUIPMENT

- measuring cups and spoons
- 2 mixing bowls • 9-inch springform pan, greased (Make sure it's in the closed position.) • electric mixer
- rubber spatula • table knife

makes 1 cake (10 to 12 slices)

ingredients

- 1 cup finely ground graham cracker crumbs
- ¼ cup sugar
- ½ stick (¼ cup) butter, melted
- 4 8-ounce packages cream cheese, softened to room temperature
- 1 cup sugar
- 1 teaspoon vanilla extract
- 4 eggs, warmed to room temperature

1. Preheat the oven to 300°F. Combine the graham cracker crumbs, ¼ cup sugar, and melted butter in a mixing bowl. Use your clean hands to mix until it feels like damp sand. Press the crumb mixture in an even layer on the bottom of the springform pan.

2. In the other bowl, cream the cream cheese and sugar with the electric mixer on medium until smooth and fluffy. Add the vanilla. Add the eggs one at a time, beating between additions. Check the variation you're making—this might be the time to add some flavor.

3. Scrape the batter onto the crust in the springform pan. Use the rubber spatula to smooth the top. Bake 60 to 65 minutes, until the middle of the cake barely moves when you jiggle the pan. Turn the oven off, but leave the cheesecake in there for another hour.

4. Chill your cake before removing it from the pan. (See what I mean about waiting?) Run a table knife between the sides of the cake and the pan to loosen the cake from the pan. Slowly flip the lever that opens the springform pan. If you notice the cake sticking anywhere, use the knife in that spot. Remove the pan. Voilà!

Want some variations?

- Mochaccino Cheesecake: Add 2 tablespoons of instant coffee when you add the eggs. Stir 1 cup semi-sweet minichocolate chips into the batter just before you scrape it into the pan.
- Raspberry Tie-Dye: After all of the eggs have been mixed into the batter, add 1 cup seedless raspberry jam. Stir until you like the look of the swirls.

Sweet & Simple Custard

This recipe pulls double duty as a dessert or a nutritious breakfast or snack. And it's really easy to make.

EQUIPMENT

• kettle full of water • measuring cups and spoons • mixing bowl or quart measuring cup with a spout • fork • ladle (optional) • 3 to 5 custard cups or a baking dish, 8 x 8 inches • baking dish large enough to hold the other baking dish(es)

makes 3 to 5 servings

ingredients

- 2 eggs
- ½ cup sugar
- 2 cups milk, heated to steaming but not boiling
- ⅛ teaspoon salt
- ¾ teaspoon vanilla
- ½ to 1 teaspoon ground nutmeg (I like lots of nutmeg.)

1. Preheat the oven to 300°F. Put the kettle on a high flame to boil. Put the custard cups, ramekins, or baking dish inside the large baking dish.

2. Lightly beat the eggs and sugar in the mixing bowl or large measuring cup. Add some of the warm milk to **temper** the eggs. Add the remaining milk, salt, and vanilla. Beat lightly until well combined.

3. Pour or ladle the egg mixture into the cups or smaller baking dish. Sprinkle nutmeg on top. Use oven mitts to pull the middle rack partially out of the oven, and set the large baking dish on it. Pour boiling water into the large dish, being careful not to get water in your custard. (The French term for this set-up is **bain marie.**) Bake for 50 to 55 minutes, or until the custard is mostly solid (the middle will still wobble a little.) Let the custard rest in the bain marie at room temperature for 15 minutes. Enjoy warm or cold.

I like to bake this recipe in individual custard cups or ramekins. If you bake it all in one dish, add 10 to 15 minutes to the cooking time.

Well-Bred Pudding

Bread pudding combines the creamy sweetness of pudding and the crunchy goodness of baked apples and bits of bread. It looks classy when you bake and serve it in individual dishes, which could be enough to convince people that you are a professional chef.

EQUIPMENT

• measuring cups and spoons • mixing bowl • fork • 4 to 6 greased custard cups or ramekins, or a greased baking dish about 8 x 8 inches • baking sheet (optional) • ladle

makes 4 to 6 servings

ingredients

- 2 eggs
- ½ cup sugar
- 2 cups milk, heated to steaming but not boiling
- ⅛ teaspoon salt
- ¾ teaspoon vanilla
- 4 cups bread, torn into bite-sized pieces
- 2 apples, peeled, cored and diced
- 1 cup raisins
- ½ teaspoon ground cinnamon

1. Preheat the oven to 325°F.

2. Lightly beat the eggs and sugar in the mixing bowl or large measuring cup. Add some of the warm milk to **temper** the eggs. Add the remaining milk, salt, and vanilla. Beat lightly until well combined. Add the bread, apples, raisins, and cinnamon. Stir to combine, then let the mixture rest for 10 minutes so the bread can soak up the liquid.

3. Ladle the pudding mixture into the cups or baking dish. If you're using individual cups, put them on a baking sheet to make it easier to move them in and out of the oven. Bake 25 to 30 minutes until **set**. Remove from the oven and let the pudding cool for just a minute or two before eating.

Ice Cream, You Scream

Dress up plain ice cream by putting it in a pie. Use any flavor you want. I chose chocolate because I'm crazy for chocolate.

EQUIPMENT

• mixing bowl • electric mixer or immersion blender • rubber spatula • plastic wrap • vegetable peeler

makes 1 pie (6 to 8 slices)

ingredients

- 1 Perfecto Pie Crust (See next page.)
- ½ gallon of your favorite ice cream
- 1 pint heavy cream (also called whipping cream)
- 2 teaspoons sugar
- ½ teaspoon vanilla extract
- maraschino cherries
- chocolate candy bar

1. Put your ice cream in the sink to soften while you make the whipped cream.

2. Combine the heavy cream, sugar, and vanilla extract in the mixing bowl. Whip until stiff. Your whipped cream is ready.

3. Fill the cooled pie crust (which you'll make using the instructions on the next page) with the softened ice cream and smooth the top with a rubber spatula. Cover the pie with plastic wrap and put it in the freezer for at least 30 minutes to firm up. (It's safe to put glass in the freezer now that it has cooled down.)

4. Serve your marvelous creation with whipped cream and cherries on top. I made chocolate curls for the top by pulling a vegetable peeler across a chocolate bar.

Perfecto Pie Crust

The key to making pie dough that's easy to work with and bakes up crisp and flaky is to keep the ingredients cold. After you measure, stick everything in the freezer for a couple of minutes.

makes 2 single-crust pies or 1 double crust

ingredients

- 2¼ cups all-purpose flour
- ¼ teaspoon salt
- ¼ teaspoon baking powder
- 1¾ sticks (7 ounces) butter, cut into chunks
- ⅓ cup super-cold water
- 1 tablespoon vinegar

1. Preheat the oven to 425°F. It's time to mix, and you can use a food processor or mix by hand.

Food Processor Method: Put the flour, salt, and baking powder into the bowl of the food processor fitted with the blade attachment. Pulse three times to combine, and then add the butter. Pulse five times, or until you see the butter's been cut into little pieces, none of them bigger than a raisin. (See photo.) Combine the water and vinegar, and add it to the flour mixture. Pulse five more times. Unplug the food processor and dump the crumbly dough into a mixing bowl. Go on to step 2.

Hand Method: Combine the flour, salt, and baking powder in the mixing bowl. Cut the butter in with the pastry blender. (See photo.) Cut until you see the butter's been cut into little pieces, none of them bigger than a raisin. Combine the water and vinegar and add it to the flour mixture. Stir lightly until the water is evenly distributed. Go on to step 2.

2. Use your hands to squeeze the dough together, kneading just until it comes together in a ball. Divide the dough in half and form each half into a disc. Wrap the discs in plastic and put them in the fridge for at least 15 minutes. (You only need one of the discs for recipes other than Razzle Dazzle Pie, so double wrap the other one and put it in the freezer. The next time you make a pie, just let this dough thaw until you can roll it out.)

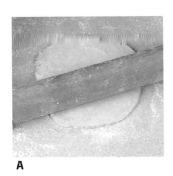
A

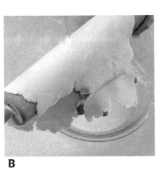
B

C

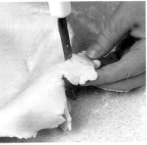
D

3. Sprinkle a little bit of flour on your pastry board and rub some on the rolling pin. Unwrap a chilled dough disc and put it on the board. Roll out the pie crust by starting in the middle and pushing the rolling pin down and away from you to the edge of the dough. (See photo A.) Give the dough a quarter turn and repeat the rolling. Keep turning and rolling until the dough is about ¼ inch thick.

4. To transfer the dough to a pie plate, roll it loosely around the rolling pin, move it over the pie plate, and unroll it into the dish. (See photos B and C.) It's important not to stretch the dough up the sides of the dish, or it will shrink when it bakes. Just ease it in. (If you're using Perfecto Pie Crust for a recipe other than Ice Cream, You Scream, turn to that recipe now.)

5. Use kitchen shears or a paring knife to trim the crust to about ½ inch from the lip of the pie plate. (See photo D.) Make a ruffled edge with two fingers and a thumb. (See photo E.) Another **crimping** method uses a fork. (See photo F.)

6. Line the inside of the pie crust with aluminum foil or parchment paper, leaving a good bit of extra hanging from the edges. Fill this with dry beans. (See photo G.) Bake 20 minutes. (This ruins the beans for eating, but you can save them to use over and over again as pie crust weights.)

7. Remove the crust from the oven, and lift the foil or paper out, taking the beans with it. Be careful because the foil and beans are really hot. Now prick the pie crust in several places with a fork. Bake 3 minutes and check it out. If the crust is puffing up anywhere, prick it with the fork some more. Bake another 5 to 10 minutes, or until golden brown.

E

F

8. Remove the pie crust from the oven. Let the pie crust cool to room temperature. Warning: If you use a glass pie plate (my favorite kind), don't try to speed up the cooling process by putting it in the freezer—the sudden temperature change could cause it to explode. Really.

G

Cherry Pie-in-the-Sky

People are always impressed by a lattice crust like this one. It looks difficult to make, but it's just a puzzle. The secret is to use super-chilled strips of dough, and to follow my directions.

makes 1 pie (6 to 8 servings)

ingredients

- 1 recipe Perfecto Pie Crust dough (page 76), prepared through step 4
- three 14.5-ounce cans of cherries, drained
- ¼ cup cornstarch
- 1½ cup sugar
- 1 teaspoon vanilla extract or ½ teaspoon almond extract
- pinch of salt
- egg wash (See page 87.) (optional)

1. Preheat the oven to 400°F. Roll out one of the rounds of dough and put it in the pie plate but don't trim or **crimp** the edges yet. (See steps 3-4 on page 77.) Stick the pie plate in the fridge.

2. Roll out the second round of dough. Using the straight edge of the ruler as a guide, cut the dough into strips about 1 inch wide. It's okay if the strips are different lengths, but try to make them all the same width. Chill the strips while you make the cherry filling.

3. Stir the cherries, cornstarch, sugar, extract of your choice, and salt together until well combined. Ta-da! Filling. Dump this into the crust in the pie plate.

4. Now for the fancy lattice top: Keep in mind that you need longer strips at the center of the pie and shorter ones at the edges. Arrange several strips of dough parallel to each other on top of the pie, leaving some space between them. Gently fold every other strip halfway back on itself. Lay a new strip of dough perpendicularly across the unfolded strips. (See photo.) Unfold the folded strips, and fold the ones that didn't get folded the first time back over the perpendicular strip. Lay down a second perpendicular strip, and unfold the other ones. Do you get how this works? Turn the pie around, and weave the other half in the same way, again starting from the center and working your way out.

5. Crimp the edges with a fork. If you want a shiny top, brush it with egg wash. Bake 50 to 55 minutes, or until the crust is golden brown and the cherry juice is bubbling and translucent. Wear the oven mitts to remove the pie from the oven. Let the pie cool a bit before slicing it. I like to eat cherry pie with vanilla ice cream.

Razzle Dazzle Pie

I added raspberries to a classic apple pie recipe, for super-charged color and flavor. I also gave this pie a top crust and cut stars out of the dough before baking it. Brilliant, right?

EQUIPMENT

• measuring cups and spoons
• mixing bowl • wooden spoon •
pastry board • rolling pin • greased
pie plate • kitchen shears or paring
knife • small cookie cutter • pastry
brush • aluminum foil

makes 1 double-crust fruit pie

ingredients

- 1 Perfecto Pie Crust (page 76)
- 4 cups peeled and sliced fruit*
- ¼ cup cornstarch
- ½ to 1½ cups sugar, depending on how sweet the fruit is
- 1 teaspoon vanilla extract
- 1 teaspoon cinnamon (optional)
- pinch salt
- egg wash (See page 87.)

  * *I used 3 cups apples and 1 cup raspberries.*

1. Preheat the oven to 400°F. Stir the fruit, cornstarch, sugar, vanilla, cinnamon, and salt together in a mixing bowl until the cornstarch dissolves. Let this mixture sit while you turn to page 76 and make your pie crust.

2. Roll out the bottom crust and put it in the pie plate as described on page 77. Dump the fruit filling into the crust.

3. Roll out the top crust. Cut several small shapes out of the dough. (This will let steam from the fruit escape during baking.) Loosely wrap the top crust around the rolling pin, and transfer it onto the pie.

4. Use kitchen shears or a paring knife to trim both layers of crust to about ½ inch from the lip of the pie plate. Make a ruffled edge with two fingers and a thumb. (See photo E on page 77.)

5. Use egg wash to glue the cut-out dough shapes on the top crust for extra decoration. If you want a shiny crust, paint the whole thing with egg wash. Bake 50 to 55 minutes, or until the crust is golden brown.

Check your pie about 30 minutes into the baking time. If the edges of the crust are already browned, carefully cover them with aluminum foil so they don't burn while the rest of the pie finishes baking.

Peanut Butter — Hold the Jelly

Did you think I'd write a baking book without a cookie recipe? Here's one of my favorites, plus three variations for extra peanut butter goodness.

EQUIPMENT

• measuring cups and spoons • mixing bowls • mixer • fork • 2 greased cookie sheets • spoon

makes about 24 cookies

ingredients

- 1 stick butter, softened at room temperature
- ½ cup granulated sugar
- ½ cup packed brown sugar
- 1 egg
- 1 teaspoon vanilla extract
- 1 cup peanut butter (crunchy or creamy, you choose)
- 1¼ cup flour
- ½ teaspoon baking soda
- ½ teaspoon salt

1. Preheat the oven to 375°F. Cream the butter and sugars in a large mixing bowl. Add the egg and vanilla to the creamed mixture. Blend well. Then add the peanut butter. Mix until smooth. (Okay, if you choose crunchy peanut butter, the mixture won't get smooth!)

2. Mix the dry ingredients in a separate bowl. Then add this mixture to the wet (peanut butter) mixture. Blend well.

3. Use your hands to roll a spoonful of dough into a ball. Place the ball on the cookie sheet. Continue until you've used all the dough.

4. Use a fork to mash each dough ball flat, first in one direction, then perpendicularly, to make a grid design. (See photo.)

5. Bake for 8 to 10 minutes. Wear the oven mitts to remove the cookie sheets from the oven. Allow the cookies to cool before eating them.

More peanut butter cookies

- Make Kiss Me cookies by placing one chocolate kiss in the center of each ball of cookie dough. (Skip the step making the grid pattern.)
- Make your cookies Extra Nutty like the cookies in the top left of the photo by adding 1 cup of mixed nuts to the original recipe.

Bread Basics

The summer when I was thirteen I made bread almost every day. I got so good at it that I didn't need to follow recipes—I just made them up! Impressive, huh? Soon everyone will be impressed when you make bread from scratch, too. This short section will show and tell you everything you need to know to make the eight bread recipes that follow in this chapter. You can also check out the sidebar on page 86 to learn how to make up your own recipes.

Ingredients

Basic bread is made from a blend of flour, yeast, and water. But if the bread is a Gotcha Focaccia on page 104, the cheeses and veggies you choose to include will make a big impact on the overall taste. No matter what kind of bread you want to make, however, the crucial ingredient is always **yeast**. That's what makes bread rise and makes for a light, delicious bread instead of a heavy, cardboard-like bread. It's important to treat the yeast right, so that it activates and starts the rising process. Begin by mixing the right way.

Proof It!

Is your yeast more than a year old? Proof it to make sure it's still alive. Put the yeast and warm water in the mixing bowl with a pinch of sugar. Does it get frothy after a few minutes? Use it. Otherwise, you need fresh yeast.

Mixing

There are lots of ways to mix the ingredients for bread dough. I use a method that starts with a **biga**. Just mix the yeast, warm liquid, sugar (if the recipe calls for it), and about half of the flour (no need to measure) in a mixing bowl. Let the biga **rest** at least ten minutes to jump start the yeast. You can let it rest longer if you like—I've left it in the fridge overnight. Biga looks swampy and bubbly after it rests.

Adjustments

Add the rest of the ingredients to the biga. Depending on the weather and the wheat used to make your flour (even the weather when the wheat was grown!), you

may need more or less flour than my recipe calls for. Leave a handful of flour in your measuring cup. Stir the ingredients together and keep adding flour until the dough is shaggy and pulls away from the sides of the bowl.

Kneading

Dump the dough onto a floured pastry board or countertop. Flour your hands too. Knead the dough by pushing it down and away from your body with the heels of

your hands, like you see above. Then fold the dough in half and give it a quarter turn, like you see below. Keep kneading. At first the dough will be floppy and sticky. Sprinkle more flour on it if it's too sticky to handle. As you knead, the dough will become smooth and springy. Look closely—you can see the long strands of **gluten** in your dough. When you think you've kneaded enough, do five more push-fold-turn combos. It's almost impossible to knead too much when you're doing it by hand.

Rising

It's time to let the yeast work while you rest your weary arms. Rinse the mixing bowl clean with hot water to warm the bowl. Pour about one teaspoon of oil into the

bowl, slop the dough around in the oil, and flip the dough over so it's oiled on both sides. (I skip the oil sometimes. It doesn't seem to make much difference, unless the weather is really dry. Oil keeps the dough from drying out while it rises. Do what makes sense in your climate.)

Cover the bowl with a clean kitchen towel, and let it rise in a warm place until it's doubled in size, usually about an hour. Check to see if your dough's done rising by poking it with your finger, like you see in the photo on the left. If the dimple stays, it's done.

Punching

I don't know why this step is called punching. If you really punched, your fist would be covered in sticky dough! Here's how it works: move

the dough from the bowl to your work surface. Then push the dough down with your fist, gently deflating it. That's it. (The dough

doesn't put up much of a fight.) Then knead a few times to give the yeast some fresh oxygen. If the recipe makes more than one loaf, now's the time to divide the dough.

Rounding

Brush the extra flour off of your work surface. Use the sides of your

hands to move the dough in a circle. Gently push down at the same time. As you round, the dough will become a smooth sphere with gluten stretched evenly over the surface. The bottom of the sphere will stick to the board a little bit and look rough. I think of that spot as the bread's belly button. (Don't be frustrated—I couldn't do it my first time either. Luckily, your bread will turn out perfectly even if your rounding doesn't.)

Forming

There are lots of ways to form loaves. This is how you do the typical kind. (Check out the recipes for other ideas.) Let the rounded dough rest for 5 to 10 minutes so

the gluten can relax. Flatten the round with your hand, and flip it over so the smooth side is down. Roll the dough into a log. Tuck the ends up, and pinch the seam closed, as you see in the photo. Put the loaf in a greased loaf pan, seam down.

Proofing

Yeah, "proof" means two different things in baking—go figure! For this kind of proofing, cover the loaves with a kitchen towel and let them **rise** in a warm place until **doubled** in size, about 45 minutes. This is just like the first rise. Start preheating the oven towards the end of proofing.

Slashing

When the yeast hits the heat of the oven, it gets very active and produces one last burst of gas, making the bread rise a little more. This is called **oven spring**. Often, the crust of the bread forms before oven spring is over. Give the loaf room to rise so it doesn't crack the crust. Just pull a serrated knife

across the top of the loaf, slicing ¼ to ¾ inch deep. It's up to you whether to make one long slash or several small ones.

Baking

Bake your bread in the center of the oven for the time recommended in the recipe. About halfway through baking, turn the loaves around to make sure they cook evenly on all sides. (To test for "doneness," you can tap the loaf on the top and see if it sounds hollow. Hollow equals done.)

The Upper Crust

For a little something extra, brush the crust of your bread before you slash it. Melted butter will keep the crust soft. Plain water will make the crust crisp and chewy, like French bread. Egg wash will make it beautifully dark and shiny. To make egg wash, crack one egg in a small bowl. Add 1 tablespoon of water. Beat with a fork. Easy, huh?

Cooling & Storage

Wearing oven mitts, flip the bread out of its pan and onto a wire **cooling rack**. The texture will be best if you let it cool before slicing, but I totally understand if you can't wait. Store cooled bread in a plastic bag at room temperature.

Baking Science

You use bread flour for making bread because it has more of the proteins that make **gluten** than all-purpose and cake flours. You knead and knead until the gluten is really long, making the dough feel smooth and springy. (Gluten also makes bread chewy.)

In many baking recipes, the challenge is NOT to let the gluten get long. (Chewy muffins? No thanks!) Recipes for tender baked goods start with low-protein flour, and add butter, oil, and/or sugar. Those ingredients block water from joining proteins, so the gluten strands stay short. (This is how shortcake got its name.) Just a little bit of mixing or kneading is all it takes to form batter or dough. (Cake batter is an exception to this rule because it doesn't have much flour.) Eggs also have proteins that contribute to the structure of baked goods.

Look closely at a slice of bread or the middle of a biscuit. Before you baked it, the dough didn't have all that air in it, right? The structure that you made by mixing and kneading trapped carbon dioxide gas that was given off by **leaveners** while your goodies baked. Leaveners include yeast, baking soda, and baking powder.

Yeast is a tiny organism that eats sugar and gives off carbon dioxide. (No sugar added to the recipe? Yeast can break flour down into sugar.) Don't get creeped out—it's alive. It's not an animal, so vegetarians don't need to avoid it. In fact, yeast is less complicated than plants. The dry yeast that you buy in the store is dormant. It needs water and warmth to do its thing. Use liquids the temperature of a warm bath—any hotter might kill the yeast. Bread dough rises because of the gas from the yeast.

Baking soda and baking powder also cause chemical reactions in your breads, but for different reasons. Baking soda is an alkaline ingredient that reacts with acidic ingredients, such as the molasses in gingerbread, to make carbon dioxide gas. If you've ever made a "volcano" with baking soda and vinegar, you know how bubbly that reaction is.

Baking powder is made of baking soda plus an acidic ingredient, for recipes that don't include another acidic ingredient. It doesn't explode in its package because it needs water and heat to activate it. That's why biscuits rise in the oven.

That's a lot of science, huh? Maybe you can use your knowledge and baking skills for a school project. Bonus points if everyone gets a taste.

Cinnamon Swirl

Want a sweet, scrumptious bread? Look no further. I recommend you slice and toast Cinnamon Swirl for one of my favorite sandwiches: peanut butter, pineapple cream cheese, and sliced apple.

makes 2 loaves

ingredients

- 2½ cups milk, heated to the temperature of a warm bath
- ½ cup sugar
- 2 packets (4½ teaspoons) active dry yeast
- about 6½ cups bread flour
- 2 tablespoons cooking oil such as canola
- 2 teaspoons salt
- 2 to 3 tablespoons ground cinnamon
- egg wash (page 87)

1. Stir the milk, sugar, yeast and about half of the flour together in the mixing bowl. Let it sit for 5 to 10 minutes until it looks swampy. Add the remaining flour, salt, and oil. Stir until you have shaggy dough, adjusting the amount of flour as needed.

2. Dump the dough onto the board and knead until springy and smooth. Rinse the mixing bowl clean with hot water, dry it, and put the dough in. Cover the dough with a clean kitchen towel and let it rise until doubled, about an hour.

3. Punch down the dough. Divide the dough in half and round each half. Let the rounds rest for 5 to 10 minutes.

4. Use the rolling pin to roll out one of the rounds into a rectangle as wide as your loaf pan is long. Sprinkle cinnamon all over the dough. Roll the rectangle up into a cylinder. (See photo.) Pinch the seam closed. Put the loaf in the loaf pan, seam side down.

5. Repeat step 4 with the other half of the dough. Cover both loaves with the kitchen towel, and let rise until doubled, about 50 minutes.

6. Preheat the oven to 350°F. Brush the loaves with egg wash, and slash them with the serrated knife. Bake 50 to 55 minutes or until they turn deep golden brown. Flip the baked bread out of the pans onto wire racks. Let the bread cool before slicing or eating it.

Stollen Goods

No, this isn't a recipe for a life of crime. It's for an Austrian bread with sweet dried fruit that's so good you might try to swipe someone else's piece. (Pronounce it "SCHTO-len.")

makes 10 to 12 servings

ingredients

- 2 eggs, lightly beaten
- ½ cup milk, heated to the temperature of a warm bath
- ⅓ cup sugar
- 1 packet (2¼ teaspoons) active dry yeast
- about 3 cups bread flour
- ½ teaspoon salt
- ½ stick (¼ cup) butter, melted
- ¼ teaspoon ground nutmeg, or a pinch of ground mace
- 1½ cups dried fruit (I use apricots, cherries, and golden raisins.)
- about ½ cup apple juice, heated until it steams
- ½ cup pecan halves
- 1 cup powdered sugar
- 2 tablespoons milk

1. Stir the eggs, milk, sugar, yeast and about half of the flour together in the mixing bowl until well blended. Let it rest for 5 minutes until it looks swampy. Add the remaining flour, salt, butter, and nutmeg. Stir until you have soft, shaggy dough, adjusting the amount of flour as needed.

2. Dump the dough onto the board and knead until springy and smooth. Rinse the mixing bowl clean with hot water, dry it, and put the dough in. Cover the dough with a clean kitchen towel and let it rise until doubled, about an hour. Meanwhile, soak the dried fruits in apple juice to make them plump and juicy. (This is called reconstituting.)

3. Preheat the oven to 350°F. Punch down the dough. Round the dough on the pastry board and let it rest for 5 to 10 minutes. While the dough is resting, drain the extra apple juice off the reconstituted fruits. Stir the pecans into the fruit—this mixture will be your filling.

4. Use the rolling pin to roll the dough out into a rectangle ¼ to ½ inch thick. Imagine that the rectangle is divided into thirds lengthwise. The middle section will stay whole. Make diagonal slices in the two outside sections, as you see in the photo. Put the filling on the middle section. Starting at the end that the slices angle away from, fold a strip of dough over the filling. Now fold over from the other side, overlapping the first strip. Keep going back and forth, folding and overlapping, until you get to the end. (See photo.) Tuck the bottom flap of dough under the braided part and pinch to seal the end.

5. Transfer the stollen to the baking sheet. Bake 35 to 40 minutes, or until golden brown. Then stir the powdered sugar and milk together with a fork. Drizzle this glaze over the baked stollen. Enjoy.

My Dilly Bread Recipe

My friend Aletha loves dilly bread. Every time she tastes some that I made she asks me if I used her mother's recipe. Um, no, it's my recipe. But I take it as a compliment because Aletha's mom is a really good cook.

EQUIPMENT

• measuring cups and spoons • chopping board • chef's knife • frying pan • spatula • mixing bowl • wooden spoon • floured pastry board • kitchen towel • 8 x 9 inch greased baking dish • pastry brush

makes 9 servings

ingredients

- 1 white onion, diced small (about 1 cup)
- ¼ stick (2 tablespoons) butter
- ¾ cup water, the temperature of a warm bath
- 2 teaspoons sugar
- 1 packet (2¼ teaspoons) active dry yeast
- 1 egg, lightly beaten
- about 3 cups bread flour
- 1 teaspoon salt
- 1 bunch fresh dill, minced (about 1 cup)
- melted butter
- about 2 teaspoons coarse salt

1. Melt the butter in the skillet on a low flame. Add the onions and **sweat** to 10 minutes, until they are soft and sort of see-through. Let this mixture cool a bit so the heat won't kill the yeast when you add the onions to the dough.

2. Stir the water, sugar, yeast, egg, and around half of the flour in the mixing bowl until well blended. Let it rest for 5 minutes until it looks swampy. Add the remaining flour, salt, dill, and onion mixture. Stir with wooden spoon until you have shaggy dough, adjusting flour as needed.

3. Dump the dough onto the board and knead until springy and smooth (except for the onion chunks, of course). Rinse the mixing bowl clean with hot water, dry it, and put the dough in. Cover the dough with a clean kitchen towel and let it rise until doubled, about an hour.

4. Punch down the dough. Divide the dough into nine equal pieces and round each piece. (See photo.) Arrange the rounds in three rows of three in the baking dish. Cover with the kitchen towel and let rise until doubled, about 45 minutes.

5. Preheat the oven to 350°F. Brush the top of the bread with melted butter. Sprinkle it with coarse salt. Bake 30 to 35 minutes, or until golden brown. Let it cool a bit before you flip it out of the baking dish. Aletha and I think My Dilly Bread is best when it's still warm from the oven.

Rockin' Rolls

My cousin Tim keeps a ball of play dough in his kitchen to remind him what size to make his rolls. It's his roll model.

makes 24 rolls

ingredients

- 2 cups water, the temperature of a warm bath
- 2 packets (4½ teaspoons) active dry yeast
- ½ cup sugar
- 1 egg, lightly beaten
- about 6½ cups bread flour
- ½ stick (¼ cup) butter, melted
- 1½ teaspoons salt
- more melted butter (optional)

1. Stir the water, yeast, sugar, egg, and about half of the flour together in the mixing bowl. Let it sit 5 to 10 minutes, until it looks swampy. Add the remaining flour, salt, and melted butter. Stir until you have shaggy dough, adjusting the amount of flour as needed.

2. Dump the dough onto the board and knead until springy and smooth. Rinse the mixing bowl clean with hot water, dry it, and put the dough in. Cover the dough with a clean kitchen towel and let it rise until doubled, about an hour.

3. Punch down the dough. Form the dough into rounds the size of walnuts. Place the rolls two inches apart on the greased baking sheet. Cover them with the kitchen towel, and let rise until doubled, about 45 minutes.

4. Preheat the oven to 350°F. Brush the rolls with melted butter if you like. Bake 30 to 35 minutes, or until golden brown. I like rolls best when they're hot.

Pita Treata

Hollow pita bread seems like magic—how'd the pocket get in there, anyway? See if you can figure it out . . .

EQUIPMENT

• measuring cups and spoons • mixing bowl • wooden spoon • floured pastry board • kitchen towel • chef's knife • rolling pin • baking sheet(s) • cooling rack

1. Stir the water, yeast, and bread flour in the mixing bowl until well blended. Let it rest 5 minutes until it looks swampy. Add the whole wheat flour, salt, and olive oil. Stir until you have shaggy dough, adjusting flour as needed.

2. Dump the dough onto the board and knead until springy and smooth. Rinse the mixing bowl clean with hot water, dry it, and put the dough in. Cover the dough with a clean kitchen towel and let it rise until doubled, about an hour.

3. Punch down the dough. Use the knife to divide the dough into 8 equal pieces and round each piece. Let the rounds rest 10 minutes.

4. Preheat the oven to 400°F. Roll out each piece of dough into a circle about ¼ inch thick. Put them on a baking sheet. (You should be able to fit two or three pitas on one baking sheet. If you only have one baking tray, it's okay to bake the pitas in batches.)

5. Bake the pitas 10 to 12 minutes, until they are puffed up and lightly browned. Then transfer the baked pitas to wire racks to cool. What do you think? Are the pitas puffed full of magic?

makes 8 pita rounds

Ingredients

- 1¼ cup water, the temperature of a warm bath
- 1 packet (2¼ teaspoons) active dry yeast
- 2 cups bread flour
- about 1¼ cup whole wheat flour
- ½ teaspoon salt
- 2 tablespoons olive oil

Confetti Bread

This colorful bread is so full of tasty, chunky ingredients, it's almost a sandwich by itself. Feel free to substitute whatever kinds of veggies you like best—there should be a total of 4 cups of diced veggies.

• cutting board • chef's knife • measuring cups and spoons • mixing bowl • wooden spoon • floured pastry board • kitchen towel • 2 greased loaf pans • serrated knife • cooling rack

makes 2 loaves

ingredients

- 3 cups water, the temperature of a warm bath
- 1 tablespoon sugar
- 2 packages (4½ teaspoons) active dry yeast
- about 6½ cups bread flour
- 2 teaspoons salt
- 2 teaspoons garlic powder
- 2 tablespoons olive oil
- 2 red bell peppers, seeded and diced
- 2 green peppers, seeded and diced
- 1 red onion, peeled and diced
- 1 pound cheddar cheese, diced

1. Stir the water, sugar, yeast and around half of the flour in the mixing bowl until well blended. Let it rest for 5 minutes, until it looks swampy. Add the remaining flour, salt, garlic powder, and olive oil. Stir until you have shaggy dough, adjusting flour as needed. Add the veggies and cheese.

2. Dump the dough onto the board and knead until springy and smooth (except for the confetti chunks, of course). Rinse the mixing bowl clean with hot water, dry it, and put the dough in. Cover the dough with a clean kitchen towel and let it rise until doubled, about an hour.

3. Punch down the dough. Divide the dough in half and round each half. Let the rounds rest for 10 minutes. Form the rounds into loaves and put them in the loaf pans. Cover with the kitchen towel and let rise until doubled, about 45 minutes.

4. Preheat the oven to 350°F. Slash the tops of the loaves with the serrated knife. Bake 45 to 50 minutes, or until deep golden brown. Then flip the loaves out of the pans and onto wire racks to cool.

Savor the Flavor

Every time I walk by the rosemary bush in my front yard I rub it to stir up the scent. It's one of the most delicious smells in the world! I put lots of rosemary in this tasty walnut bread.

EQUIPMENT

- measuring cups and spoons
- mixing bowl • wooden spoon
- floured pastry board • kitchen towel
- rolling pin • 2 greased baking sheets
- serrated knife • cooling rack

1. Stir the water, yeast, and bread flour together in the mixing bowl. Let it sit 5 to 10 minutes, until it looks swampy. Add the remaining ingredients. Stir until you have shaggy dough, adjusting the amount of flour as needed.

2. Dump the dough onto the board and knead until springy and smooth (except for the lumpy walnuts, of course). Rinse the mixing bowl clean with hot water, dry it, and put the dough in. Cover the dough with a clean kitchen towel and let it rise until doubled, about an hour.

3. Punch down the dough. Divide the dough in half and round each half. Place each round on a baking sheet, and cover with the kitchen towel. Let rise until doubled, about 50 minutes.

4. Preheat the oven to 350°F. Slash an X in each loaf with the serrated knife. Bake 45 to 50 minutes, until deep brown. Let the baked bread cool on wire racks.

makes 2 round loaves

ingredients

- 1 packet (2¼ teaspoons) active dry yeast
- 1¼ cup water, the temperature of a warm bath
- 2 cups bread flour
- about 1½ cups whole wheat flour
- ½ teaspoon salt
- ¼ cup olive oil
- ¼ cup fresh rosemary leaves
- 1 cup walnut pieces
- 1 onion, diced small (about 1 cup) (optional)

Gotcha Focaccia

Can you resist yummy Italian bread sprinkled with cheese and your favorite veggies? Most people are hooked on focaccia after the first bite. Maybe that's because it tastes great hot or cold, as a snack, or sliced and stuffed like a sandwich.

makes 8 to 10 servings

ingredients

- 1¼ cup water, the temperature of a warm bath
- 1 packet (2¼ teaspoons) active dry yeast
- 3 cups bread flour
- ½ teaspoon salt
- ½ teaspoon garlic powder
- 1 teaspoon Italian herbs
- ¼ cup olive oil, plus more for drizzling
- ¼ cup shredded Parmesan cheese
- toppings of your choice (I use sliced yellow squash, purple onion, and red bell pepper.)

1. Stir the water, yeast, and around half of the flour in the mixing bowl until well blended. Let it rest for 5 minutes until it looks swampy. Add the remaining flour, salt, garlic powder, herbs, and olive oil. Stir until you have shaggy dough. (It will be softer and wetter than other dough recipes in this book.)

2. Dump the dough onto the board and knead until smooth, but still floppy. (If your dough is too wet to knead the normal way, leave it in the bowl and knead it in there.) Rinse the mixing bowl clean with hot water, dry it, and put the dough in. Cover the dough with a clean kitchen towel and let it rise until doubled, about an hour.

3. Preheat the oven to 400°F. Drizzle about 1 tablespoon of olive oil onto the baking sheet and spread it around with your hands. Punch down the dough and put it on the baking sheet. Drizzle a little more oil on top, and use your greasy hands to rub the dough into an even thickness. Don't worry if the dough won't stretch all the way to the edges of the baking sheet—the rustic look makes it more authentic.

4. Dimple the surface of the dough by poking it with your finger all over, let's say twenty times. (See photo.) Sprinkle the Parmesan and toppings on the dough. Bake 20 to 25 minutes, or until the bread turns golden brown. Let your focaccia cool a little before you slice it to eat.

Equipment Glossary

Serrated knife

Vegetable peeler

Corer

Chef's knife

Paring knife

Measuring spoons

Scoop (dry) measuring cups

Liquid measuring cup

Sifter

Pastry brush

Whisk

Pastry blender

Wooden spoons

Cutting/pastry boards

Rubber spatulas

Colander

Baking dish

Electric mixer

Box grater

Pots

Mixing bowls

Food processor

Skillet

Spatula

Equipment Glossary (107)

Glossary

Bain marie: French term for "water bath." A dish of delicate food, such as custard, is placed in a larger pan of hot water while it cooks. The water keeps the temperature even so the custard doesn't curdle.

Bake: cook in an oven. When the oven is set on "bake" the heat comes from the bottom of the oven and cooks food evenly from all sides.

Baking powder: a very strong dry ingredient. Read each recipe carefully—some use baking powder and some use baking soda. They are not the same thing!

Baking rack: the wire shelf in the oven.

Baking soda: a very strong dry ingredient that makes food puff up when it bakes. The scientific term for baking soda is sodium bicarbonate.

Batter: a gloppy, wet mixture of ingredients.

Beat: stir kind of fast with a fork, electric mixer, or whisk until well combined and a little bit fluffy.

Beaters: attachments for hand-held electric mixers. I like to lick the beaters after I've made icing.

Biga: a swampy mixture of flour, water, and yeast; the first step in many of my bread recipes.

Biscuit cutters: tools you use to cut out biscuits from biscuit dough. I think metal cutters work the best.

Blade: the sharp part of a knife, blender, or food processor, which does the cutting.

Blend: to mix until well combined.

Bundt pan: a type of cake pan that makes a ring-shaped cake.

Chef's knife: a basic, big knife. See photo on page 106.

Chill: If making dough starts to stress you out, you need to chill. Really. Putting dough in the refrigerator makes it easier to work with, which can be helpful when you are making a pie crust. Chilling also slows down rising bread dough (in case you don't have time to finish right now), and encourages cheesecake to become firm.

Chunks: big (about 1½ inches square) pieces of chopped food. Chunks don't have to be perfect.

Colander: a piece of kitchen equipment that looks like a bowl with holes in it, used to rinse or drain foods. See page 107 for a photo.

Combine: stir ingredients together until they're evenly distributed.

Cored: describes a fruit whose tough middle section and seeds have been removed.

Corer: a tool used to core a piece of fruit. See page 106 for a photo.

Cream: beat together softened butter and sugar. You could do this with a fork, but using an electric mixer is much easier and quicker. See page 13 for a how-to photo.

Crimp: finishing the edges of a pie crust so your pie looks as good as it tastes. Use a fork or your fingers. See page 77 for a how-to photo.

Crumb layer: a thin layer of icing that traps cake crumbs. See page 66.

Culinary: about food. I went to culinary school to learn all about food.

Curdle: when proteins cook in clumps, like scrambled eggs.

Cutting board: a tool that protects your countertop from being cut by a knife. See page 107 for photos.

Dicing: using a knife to cut food into cubes about half an inch on each side. See page 12 for a how-to photo.

Double: when dough has yeast in it and you give it enough time, it will double in size. Or, to multiply the ingredients by 2 to make twice as much food. You don't need to change the baking time or temperature on a double batch.

Dough: the raw mixture of ingredients that will become delicious food when you bake it.

Drain: pour the juice out of canned food. You can use a strainer, or hold the lid of the can against the food while you pour.

Dredge: coating a piece of food in flour or a seasoning mixture. See page 43 for a how to photo.

Dry ingredients: ingredients that aren't wet, such as flour and salt.

Egg wash: a hand-mixed blend of egg and a little bit of water. If you brush it on the top of a pie crust or other dough before baking, the finished food will shine. See page 87 for a how-to photo.

Electric mixer: a great tool for mixing that keeps your arm from getting tired.

Equipment: another word for tools.

F: the abbreviation for Fahrenheit, which is how most American ovens measure temperature.

Flour: powdery ingredient made from wheat. "To flour" means to prepare a greased pan for baking by sprinkling flour on it. See page 15 for a how-to photo.

Fold: gently incorporate an ingredient into fluffy batter using a rubber spatula. See page 14.

Form: make something into a new shape.

Ganache: an incredibly delicious mixture of chocolate and cream.

Gluten: a long protein made of wheat proteins (mainly glutenin and gliadin) plus water. Read about how gluten works on page 88.

Grater: a tool with small, sharp holes. You rub food (such as cheese) against a grater to cut the food into small pieces. See page 107 for a photo of a box grater.

Grating: using a grater to cut small pieces of food.

Grease: rubbing butter or oil on a baking pan so the food won't stick to it. I like to use the leftover butter wrapper for this.

Halving: cutting something into two equal pieces. You can also halve a recipe by dividing the ingredients by 2.

Ingredients: all the different foods that go into a recipe.

Knead: push the dough with the heels of your hands, and then fold the dough in half. See page 14 for a how-to photo.

Knife: a tool for cutting. There's a handle and a blade—confusing the two leads to tragedy. See page 106 for photos of knives.

Leavener: an ingredient such as yeast, baking powder, or baking soda, that makes baked goods rise. See page 88 to learn how leaveners work.

Measuring cups and spoons: tools for getting the perfect amount of ingredients.

Metal spatula: a flat utensil with a handle that you use to move hot food. See photo on page 107.

Microwave: cooking something in a microwave oven.

Mincing: cutting food into tiny pieces with a knife. See page 12 for a how-to photo.

Mixing bowls: um, I think you probably know what mixing bowls are. Those round things that you put stuff in? See photo on page 107.

Oven spring: the last bit of rising that a loaf of bread does when the yeast feels the heat of the oven.

Oz: abbreviation for ounce or ounces. 2T = 1oz, and 8oz = 1 cup.

Pack: to squish an ingredient down into the measuring cup as you fill it. Brown sugar is typically packed when measuring it, but flour or other dry ingredients are not. See page 13 for a how-to photo.

Paring knife: a small knife that's good for tiny, precise cuts. See photo on page 106. "Paring" means cutting the peel off of a fruit or vegetable, but I prefer a vegetable peeler for that job.

Pastry blender: a tool for cutting butter into flour. See photo on page 106.

Pastry board: a flat surface on which you knead and roll out dough. No special equipment is needed—just use a cutting board. See photo on page 107.

Pastry brush: a paint brush for food. See photo on page 106.

Peel: to remove the skin of fruits and veggies.

Picked/picked over: to have removed stems, bad pieces, or anything else you don't want to eat from a piece of fruit, such as berries

Preheat: letting the oven heat up to the right temperature before you bake in it. Some ovens have a preheat setting, but with most of them you just turn it to bake.

Produce: fresh fruits and vegetables.

Proof: the second time bread rises. (See page 87.) Also, proof is the process of testing yeast to make sure it's still alive. (See page 85.) I know it's confusing that the same word means two different things!

Punch: deflate bread dough after it rises. It's not as violent as it sounds. See page 86 for a how-to photo.

Ramekins: baking dishes sized for individual servings. See examples in the recipe photos on pages 71 and 72.

Recipe: a plan for making food.

Reconstituting: soaking dried fruit in liquid so it gets plump and juicy.

Rest: everyone needs a little down time now and then. Even dough needs to relax!

Rise: when dough gets bigger because of leaveners. See page 86.

Rolling pin: a tool for flattening dough. See photo on page 107.

Roll out: use a rolling pin to flatten dough. See page 14.

Round: for bread dough, form the dough into a spherical shape as instructed on page 86. For other doughs, a round is a disc of dough.

Rubber spatula: a very useful spreading utensil. See photo on page 107.

Second rise: see Proofing.

Serrated knife: a knife with a saw-like blade, perfect for slicing bread. See photo on page 106.

Shaggy dough: the ingredients are combined and gluten is starting to develop. See photo on page 85.

Sift/sifted: my least favorite part of baking, where you push powdery ingredients through a sifter. If the recipe says "2 cups flour, sifted," sift after you measure. If it says "2 cups sifted flour," sift before you measure.

Sifter: a tool for sifting. See photo on page 106.

Slash: cut a shallow design in the top of a loaf of bread so it doesn't crack from oven spring. See page 87. Slashing also lets steam escape from filled pastries.

Slicing: cutting food into thin, flat pieces with a knife. See page 12 for a how-to photo.

Soften: to let an ingredient, such as butter, warm up to room temperature so it's squishy and easy to work with. Don't skip this important step.

Springform pan: a type of cake pan with a removable bottom. If a recipe calls for this kind of pan, you cannot substitute any other pan. Sorry!

Stir: use a spoon to combine ingredients.

Substitution: using a different ingredient than the recipe calls for.

Swampy dough: what the biga looks like after the yeast starts working.

Sweat: cooking veggies (usually onions) in a skillet to make them release their juices.

T: abbreviation for tablespoon.

Tablespoon: a measurement that equals ½ ounce or 3 teaspoons.

Teaspoon: a measurement that equals ⅓ tablespoon.

Temper: add a little bit of a hot mixture to beaten eggs before adding the eggs to the whole mixture, so they don't curdle. See page 31 for a photo.

Timer: an alarm that reminds you when to take your baked goods out of the oven.

Toaster oven: a miniature oven perfect for cooking small amounts of food.

tsp: abbreviation for teaspoon.

Utensils: small tools with handles.

Vegetable peeler: a tool that removes the peel of thin-skinned fruits and veggies. See photo on page 106.

Wet ingredients: ingredients that aren't dry, such as eggs and milk.

Whip: mixing very fast to make something super-fluffy, like icing. See page 13 for a how-to photo.

Whisk: the name of a tool, and the action of using it; whisking uses a wrist motion to beat and/or smooth out lumps. See tool photo on page 106.

Wire cooling rack: a tray that you put hot cookies on so they can cool off.

Yeast: the leavener used in bread dough. Read about how yeast works on page 88.

Yield: the number of servings that a recipe makes.

Zest: the colored part of the peel of a citrus fruit like oranges or lemons.

Acknowledgments

For the gorgeous photographs, all credit goes to Steve Mann. You did it again! Thank you to our models, Alex, Sam, Ben, Lacey, Twana, India, Sarah, Claire, Chelsea, Rabb Scott, Django, Lucy, and Marcus. Special thanks to Chris and Skip for the use of their home for on-location photography. Cheers to everyone at Lark Books who helped make sure no leftovers from our photo shoot were wasted. Quintuple thanks to the amazing Veronika.

Index

Metrics

Need to convert the measurements in this book to metrics? Here's how:

To convert degrees Fahrenheit to degrees Celsius, subtract 32 and then multiply by .56.

To convert inches to centimeters, multiply by 2.5.

To convert ounces to grams, multiply by 28.

To convert teaspoons to milliliters, multiply by 5.

To convert tablespoons to milliliters, multiply by 15.

To convert cups to liters, multiply by .24.

Like this book? Check out my other cookbooks.

Models Twana and Alex (pictured left) are getting thirsty admiring themselves in Delicious Drinks to Sip, Slurp, Gulp & Guzzle. It's full of easy recipes for smoothies, slushies, shakes, and more. I've included some interesting drinks from other cultures so you can expand your slurping horizons.

Big Snacks, Little Meals: After School, Dinnertime, Anytime will help you satisfy your cravings, whether they're for sweet, spicy, or something in between. Munch out on everything from light snacks like seasoned popcorn to hearty one-dish meals including a spaghetti pie—and make it all yourself!

Ready to move beyond good old PB&J? Super Sandwiches: Wrap 'Em , Stack 'Em , Stuff 'Em is for you. It's got classic sandwiches, trendy sandwiches, and sandwiches you've never heard of because I invented them just for this book. I included recipes that are great for breakfast, lunch, dinner, and snacking.

If you've been bitten by the baking bug, try my scrumptious recipes in The Greatest Cookies Ever: Dozens of Delicious, Chewy, Chunky, Fun & Foolproof Recipes. Many of the cookies are like art projects, for ultimate play-with-your-food fun. Every recipe tastes great and is easy to make.

DISABILITY AWARENESS IN THE CLASSROOM

A Resource Tool for Teachers and Students

By **LORIE LEVISON**

and **ISABELLE St. ONGE**

CHARLES C THOMAS • PUBLISHER, LTD. • SPRINGFIELD • ILLINOIS • U.S.A.